PRESIDENTS OF A DIVIDED NATION

A SOURCEBOOK ON THE U.S. PRESIDENCY

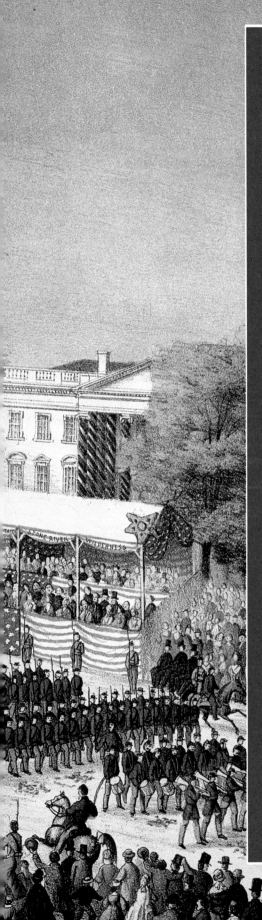

PRESIDENTS
OF A DIVIDED
NATION

A SOURCEBOOK ON THE U.S. PRESIDENCY

Edited by Carter Smith

AMERICAN ALBUMS FROM THE COLLECTIONS OF

THE LIBRARY OF CONGRESS

THE MILLBROOK PRESS, *Brookfield, Connecticut*

Cover: Abraham Lincoln meeting with General George McClellan and other officers of the Army of the Potomac. Black-and-white photograph taken for Mathew Brady by Alexander Gardner, 1862.

Title Page: "Grand Review at Washington, May 23, 1865." Lithograph published by C. Bhon, 1865.

Contents Page: "All Hail to the Flag of Freedom." Music cover, 1861.

Back Cover: "Grant's Tobacco." Lithograph, nineteenth century.

Library of Congress Cataloging-in-Publication Data

Presidents of a divided nation : a sourcebook on the U.S. presidency / edited by Carter Smith.
    p. cm. — (American albums from the collections of the Library of Congress)
    Includes bibliographical references and index.
    Summary: Uses a variety of contemporary materials to describe and illustrate the political and personal lives of the United States presidents from Abraham Lincoln to Ulysses S. Grant.
    ISBN 1-56294-360-X (lib. bdg.)
    1. Presidents—United States—History—19th century—Juvenile literature. 2. Presidents—United States—History—19th century—Sources—Juvenile literature. 3. United States—Politics and government—Civil War, 1861–1865—Juvenile literature. 4. United States—Politics and government—Civil War, 1861–1865—Sources—Juvenile literature. 5. United States—Politics and government—1865–1877—Juvenile literature. 6. United States—Politics and government—1865–1877—Sources—Juvenile literature. [1. Presidents—Sources. 2. United States—Politics and government—Civil War, 1861–1865—Sources. 3. United States—Politics and government—1865–1877—Sources.]
I. Smith, C. Carter. II. Series.
E176.1.P925 1993
973.8'092'2—dc20
[B]
                                                  93-12753
                                                     CIP
                                                       AC

 Created in association with Media Projects Incorporated

C. Carter Smith, *Executive Editor*
Lelia Wardwell, *Managing Editor*
Charles A. Wills, *Principal Writer*
Lydia Link, *Designer*
Athena Angelos, *Photo Researcher*
John Kern, *Researcher*

The consultation of Bernard F. Reilly, Jr., Head Curator of the Prints and Photographs Division of the Library of Congress, is gratefully acknowledged.

Copyright © 1993 by The Millbrook Press

Manufactured in the United States of America.

10 9 8 7 6 5 4 3 2 1

Contents

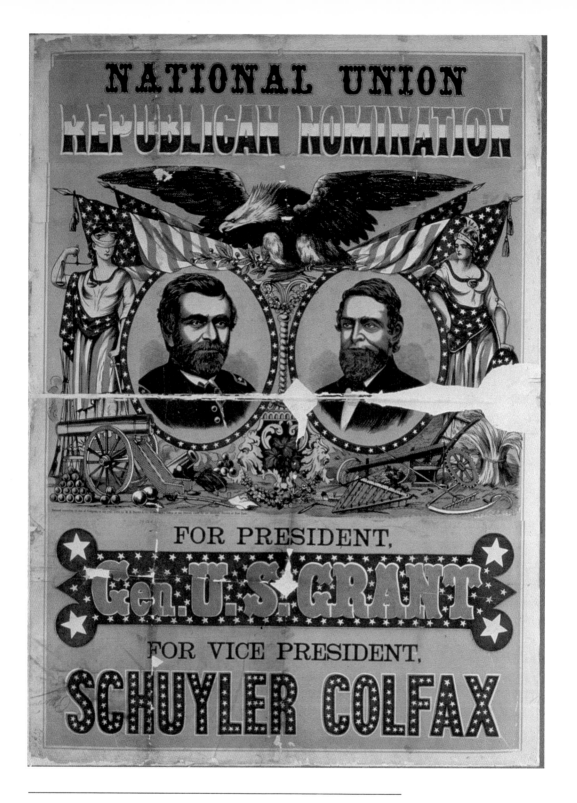

This campaign poster from the election of 1868 is decorated with portraits of Republican candidate Ulysses S. Grant and his running mate, Speaker of the House Schuyler Colfax.

Introduction

PRESENTS OF A DIVIDED NATION is one volume in a series published by The Millbrook Press titled AMERICAN ALBUMS FROM THE COLLECTIONS OF THE LIBRARY OF CONGRESS and the third of six books in the series, SOURCEBOOKS ON THE U.S. PRESIDENCY. This series chronicles the American presidency from George Washington to Bill Clinton.

The popular prints, broadsides, banners, and other ephemera reproduced in this volume reveal a great deal about how nineteenth-century Americans perceived the presidency, those that occupied that office, and those who aspired to it. Almost from the start, Americans have been intensely interested in every aspect of the lives of the presidents, both private and public. The popular prints of the nineteenth century reflect the curiosity that citizens had about the birthplaces, boyhood homes, wives, and families of the chief executive. For those presidents who were also war heroes, such as Ulysses S. Grant, their military exploits were often more widely known than their political accomplishments.

This interest extended to presidential candidates as well. And then, as today, election campaigns could be occasions for airing not only the proud, but also the embarrassing moments from a candidate's career, as the political satires of the era show. In 1860, Stephen Douglas became the first presidential candidate to take to the campaign trail himself. At the time it was considered demeaning for presidential candidates themselves to campaign, the proverbial "stump" being considered the province of demagogues and local bosses. Douglas was widely criticized in political caricatures for his departure from the norm.

The art of electioneering advanced considerably during the period covered by this volume. The election campaign of 1860 introduced the carefully orchestrated pageantry of marching clubs like New York's "Wide-Awakes," the party-organized shows of strength on a scale hitherto unheard of.

The works reproduced in PRESIDENTS OF A DIVIDED NATION represent a small but telling portion of this rich record of the history of the American presidency. These are preserved for us today by the Library of Congress in its role as the nation's library.

BERNARD F. REILLY, JR.

The United States underwent great territorial changes during the presidencies of Abraham Lincoln, Andrew Johnson, and Ulysses S. Grant. By the time Lincoln took office, in March 1861, several Southern states had seceded—withdrawn from the Union—in reaction to his election. These states, as shown on this map, formed the Confederate States of America and chose Jefferson Davis as their president. Eventually, the Confederacy included eleven states, with a total population of 9 million people, including 3 million slaves.

After four years of bitter civil war, the Confederacy was defeated by the Union, the slaves were freed, and once again one flag flew over the nation. During the war years, two new states were added. These were West Virginia, formed from Virginia's western, pro-Union counties in 1863, and a Western state, Nevada, which was admitted to the Union in 1864.

After the Civil War, the pace of Western expansion picked up. More people headed West, drawn by the Homestead Act of 1862, which gave grants of land to those willing to settle on it. The completion of the first railroad to the Pacific in 1869 made it easier to move into the territories of the West. By the end of President Grant's administration in 1877, two more Western territories had become states—Nebraska (1867) and Colorado (1876). Another territorial gain was the vast territory of Alaska, purchased from Russia in 1867, during Andrew Johnson's presidency. When America celebrated its centennial in 1876, the original thirteen states had grown to thirty-eight.

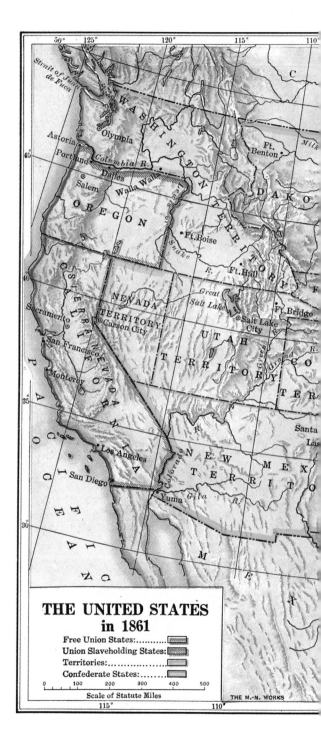

THE UNITED STATES in 1861

Free Union States:..............
Union Slaveholding States:
Territories:......................
Confederate States:..........

0   100   200   300   400   500

Scale of Statute Miles

THE M.-N. WORKS

9

A TIMELINE OF MAJOR EVENTS
1861–1864

THE PRESIDENCY

March 4, 1861 Abraham Lincoln becomes the 16th president of the United States. In his inaugural address, he appeals to the seceded states to rejoin the Union, but warns that the government will "hold, occupy, and possess" federal property in the Confederacy. War between the North and South appears to be inevitable at the start of Lincoln's presidency.

April 12 Confederate forces shell Fort Sumter in Charleston Harbor, beginning the Civil War. President Lincoln calls for 75,000 volunteers and proclaims a naval blockade of Southern ports.

September 22, 1862 Lincoln issues the Emancipation Proclamation, which will free all slaves in the Confederacy beginning the following year.

January 1, 1863 The Emancipation Proclamation becomes law. Although the decree frees no slaves immediately, it makes abolition one of the Union's war goals.

March 10 In an effort to discourage soldiers from deserting the Union Army, President Lincoln issues a proclamation stating that deserters who return to duty by April 1 will not be

Abraham Lincoln

punished. (Punishment for desertion is often death by firing squad in both the Confederate and Union armies.)

THE AMERICAN SCENE

1861 Telegraph wires are strung between New York City and San Francisco, making coast-to-coast communication possible and putting the Pony Express out of business.

February 8–9 The Confederate States of America is established, with former Secretary of War Jefferson Davis as president and Alexander Stephens as vice president.

March 9 The Confederate *Merrimack* and the Union *Monitor* clash in the first battle between armored gunboats; neither ship wins a decisive victory.

April 18 Robert E. Lee is offered command of the Union Army by general in chief Winfield Scott. Lee, a native of Virginia, refuses and later is appointed military commander of the Confederate forces.

September 17 Over 25,000 soldiers are killed, wounded, or captured at the Battle of Antietam, in Maryland, on the bloodiest day of the war.

1863 Dr. Mary Walker, a surgeon, becomes the first woman to receive an officer's commission in the U.S. Army.

March 3 To help pay for the war, Congress passes a law which authorizes the treasury to issue paper money.

• Congress passes a law authorizing conscription (the draft). The law is full of loopholes, including one which allows wealthy men to avoid the draft either by paying a fee or by hiring a substitute.

June 29 In perhaps the largest mass escape during the war, 6,000 slaves (along with nearly 5,000 mules, horses, and cattle) safely reach the Union lines in Louisiana.

November 19 Lincoln makes a brief speech at the dedication of the National Cemetery at Gettysburg. The Gettysburg Address becomes one of the most enduring presidential speeches ever delivered, but many people—including Lincoln himself—considered it a failure.

December 8 Looking toward the end of the war, Lincoln announces that he will give amnesty to all Confederates who agree to free their slaves and take an oath of loyalty to the United States.

February 9, 1864 Several photographs of President Lincoln are taken at a Washington studio. One of the photographs will become the model for the Lincoln portrait on the five dollar bill.

May 31 Republicans opposed to Lincoln nominate General John C. Frémont for president at their convention in Cleveland, Ohio.

June 7–8 The National Union Convention, made up of Republicans and pro-war Democrats, nominates Lincoln for a second presidential term. His running mate is Andrew Johnson, military governor of Tennessee.

July 4 President Lincoln vetoes the Wade-Davis Reconstruction Bill, which proposes harsh penalties on the South if a Union victory is achieved.

July 20 Lincoln watches as Union troops defend Fort Stevens, on the outskirts of Washington, from an attack by General Jubal Early's Confederate raiders.

September 2 General William Tecumseh Sherman captures Atlanta. The victory boosts Northern spirits and bolsters Lincoln's chances of reelection.

New York City draft riot

July 1–3 The Battle of Gettysburg takes place in Pennsylvania; the Union suffers 23,000 casualties, but wins the three-day battle. This conflict helps turn the tide of the war toward the Union.

July 4 Ulysses S. Grant captures the Confederate stronghold at Vicksburg, giving the Union almost complete control of the Mississippi River and severing the South's link with the West.

July 13 Anger with the federal draft law explodes into bloody rioting in New York City. The rioters, mostly Irish immigrants, turn their rage against the city's blacks, whom they believe are responsible for the war.

September 19, 1864 General Philip Sheridan wins a major victory at Winchester in Virginia's Shenandoah Valley. Sheridan destroys the farms in the valley to deny crops and cattle to the Confederacy.

November 16 Union general William Tecumseh Sherman's forces leave from Atlanta on a march through Georgia, devastating the South's resources and its capacity to wage war. Sherman captures Savannah, one of the Confederacy's few remaining ports, in December. He then turns North to invade the Carolinas.

A TIMELINE OF MAJOR EVENTS
1865–1867

THE PRESIDENCY

February 3, 1865 Lincoln and Secretary of State Seward meet with Confederate vice president Alexander Stephens aboard a ship off Hampton Roads, Virginia. The talks fail to make any progress toward a negotiated peace.

February 12 The first official observance of President Abraham Lincoln's birthday takes place in Washington, D.C. (Lincoln's birthday will become a federal holiday in 1892.)

March Congress passes the Tenure of Office Act, which requires the president to get the Senate's permission before dismissing federal officials (such as cabinet members) whose original appointments were approved by the Senate.

March 4 After defeating Democratic challenger George B. McClellan in the 1864 presidential election, Lincoln is inaugurated for a second term as president. In a moving inaugural address, he announces a moderate peace policy toward the soon-to-be-defeated Confederacy.

April 4 Just hours after the city's fall, Lincoln tours Richmond with a small escort of sailors and black soldiers. Among the sites Lincoln visits is Jefferson Davis's home. Although the city lies in ruins, Jefferson Davis urges Southerners to continue the fight against the Union. The fugitive leader of the Confederacy is captured in May by federal troops near Irwinville, Georgia. He is sentenced to two years in federal prison and released in 1867.

April 15 Lincoln dies after being shot the previous evening

THE AMERICAN SCENE

March 3, 1865 Congress authorizes the Freedmen's Bureau. The agency's purpose is to help former slaves make the transition to freedom in the Confederacy.

April 9 Confederate general Robert E. Lee surrenders to Union General Ulysses S. Grant at the Appomattox Court House in Virginia, finally ending the Civil War.

December 18 The Thirteenth Amendment to the Constitution is ratified (approved by the states), and slavery is officially abolished.

1866 Confederate veterans establish the Ku Klux Klan in Pulaski, Tennessee. The secret organization will conduct a reign of terror against former slaves and supporters of federal Reconstruction policies.
• The first of the great cattle drives brings longhorn cattle from Texas north to Abilene, Kansas, for shipment by rail to the slaughterhouses of Chicago.
• More than 50,000 people die from a cholera epidemic that sweeps the United States.

Freedmen's Bureau school

The ruins of Richmond, Virginia

by pro-Confederate actor John Wilkes Booth at Ford's Theatre. Vice President Andrew Johnson is sworn in as president.

May 29 President Johnson outlines his Reconstruction plans, which include a full pardon to those former Confederates who agree to take an oath of allegiance to the United States.

April, 1866 Congress enacts the Civil Rights Act of 1866. The law guarantees citizenship and "full and equal benefits of all laws" to African Americans.

November The congressional elections of 1866–67 strengthen the Radical Republicans' control of Congress. The new Congress is hostile to President Andrew Johnson, whom they consider to be too lenient on the formerly rebellious Southern states.

March, 1867 Congress passes the first Reconstruction Act. The law puts the South under military rule and calls for the adoption of new state constitutions in the former Confederacy.

July Congress overrides Johnson again to pass a second Reconstruction Act; this one allows the South's military governments to decide who is eligible to vote.

May 10 Supporters of women's rights hold a convention in New York City and organize the American Equal Rights Association. Their chief goal is to win the vote for women.

July 27 The first successful transatlantic telegraph cable is completed. The cable, which links the United States and Britain, is the result of a twelve-year effort by financiers Cyrus Field and Peter Cooper.

1867 The Patrons of Husbandry (later known as the Grange) is founded by Minnesota farmer Oliver H. Kelley. The Grange, which eventually numbers more than 800,000 members, works to protect farmers from exploitation by railroads, grain merchants, and other commercial interests.
• Horatio Alger publishes *Ragged Dick*, the first in a series of popular novels that promotes the virtues of hard work and clean, honest living.

January 21 Congress grants the vote to males twenty-one years or older in U.S. territories, regardless of race. African-American men also win the right to vote in Washington, D.C.

March 2 Nebraska is admitted to the Union as the thirty-seventh state.

April 9 After strong efforts by Secretary of State William Seward, Congress ratifies a treaty to purchase Alaska from Russia and appropriates $7.2 million for payment. The value of the territory is unrecognized, and Alaska is nicknamed "Seward's Folly."

June Christopher Sholes of Connecticut is granted a patent for his typewriter, which is the first truly functional model.

A TIMELINE OF MAJOR EVENTS
1868–1871

THE PRESIDENCY

1868 Citing a violation of the 1867 Tenure of Office Act, Congress impeaches President Johnson after he fires Secretary of War Edwin Stanton. Johnson is tried by the Senate and then acquitted by one vote in the first impeachment trial in American presidential history.
• The presidential election pits Union war hero Ulysses S. Grant, the Republican nominee,

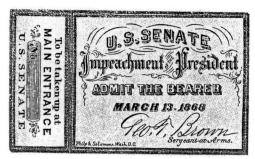

Ticket to Senate impeachment hearings

against reluctant Democratic candidate Horatio Seymour in a campaign that focuses on Reconstruction. Grant is victorious and becomes the eighteenth president of the United States.

December 25 In one of his last major actions as president, Andrew Johnson grants amnesty for all but 300 former members of the Confederate government and military.

September 24, 1869 President Grant orders the federal treasury to sell $4 million worth of gold, causing the price of gold to fall and contributing to the financial disaster dubbed "Black Friday."

January 10, 1870 President Grant asks the Senate to approve a treaty annexing the Dominican Republic in the Caribbean to the United States. The Senate rejects the treaty in June.

THE AMERICAN SCENE

1868 The Treaty of Fort Laramie ends Red Cloud's War, a two-year conflict between the U.S. Army and the Sioux Indians of the Great Plains. In a rare Indian victory, the U.S. Army agrees to abandon forts in Sioux territory, on the Bozeman Trail.

July 28 The Fourteenth Amendment is ratified. It strengthens the Civil Rights Act of 1866 by declaring former slaves to be citizens and authorizing federal protection of their rights.

1869 George Westinghouse patents the air brake, an invention which greatly improves railroad safety.
• James Oliver patents the chilled-iron plow, which breaks through tough prairie soil without clogging; this invention revolutionizes farming

in the West and Midwest.

January The National Convention of Colored Men is organized in Washington, D.C. The organization, which aims to protect the right to vote and promote education for African Americans, elects Frederick Douglass as its first president.

February 27 Congress adopts the Fifteenth Amendment, which gives black males

the right to vote in both the Northern and the Southern states.

March The Cincinnati Red Stockings, the first professional baseball team, is organized in Cincinnati, Ohio. (In November 1869 the first intercollegiate college football game, between Rutgers and Princeton, is played in New Brunswick, New Jersey.)

May 10 The last spike of the

February 7 President Grant appoints two new justices to the Supreme Court. (The Judiciary Act, passed by Congress the year before, had raised the number of justices from seven to nine.)

March 3 President Grant establishes the Civil Service Commission to ensure fairness in hiring for federal jobs.

June 13 After a rebellion against Spanish rule

Ku Klux Klan

begins in Cuba, President Grant declares that the U.S. will remain neutral.

March 3, 1871 President Grant creates the first

Civil Service Commission in an effort to promote fairness in hiring for government jobs.

• President Grant begins passing the Klu Klux Klan Acts. The Acts suspend the writ of habeas corpus—a protection against unlawful imprisonment—in some sections of the South and allow federal troops to arrest and imprison hundreds of Klansmen. Despite these efforts, the movement continues.

May American and British diplomats sign the Treaty of Washington, one of President Grant's greatest successes. It calls for an international court to decide if Britain should pay the U.S. for shipping losses caused by British-built Confederate warships. In September, Britain agrees to pay the U.S. $15 million.

First African Americans to serve in Congress

transcontinental railroad is driven in near Promontory Point, Utah Territory.

September 24 Financiers Jay Gould and Jim Fisk attempt to corner the gold

market. The result is "Black Friday"— a day of panic during which many Wall Street investors go bankrupt.

December 10 Wyoming becomes the first American

territory to allow women to vote.

1870 The census counts the nation's population at close to 40 million, a 20 percent increase from 1860.
• Senator Hiram R. Revels of Mississippi and Representative Joseph H. Rainey of South Carolina become the first black members of Congress.
• Utah becomes the second territory to give women the right to vote.

December 14 A massive fire devastates Chicago. The disaster kills more than 200 people and leaves 100,000 homeless. Property damage reaches almost $200 million.

December For the first time in ten years, all the states are represented in Congress.

A TIMELINE OF MAJOR EVENTS
1872–1878

THE PRESIDENCY

1872 A group of moderates breaks away from the Republican Party to form the Liberal Republican Party, which nominates *New York Tribune* editor Horace Greeley for president. Greeley is also the Democratic Party's nominee.
• News of the Crédit Mobilier scandal breaks just before the presidential election. The scandal involves bribes from the Union Pacific Railroad to influence prominent Republican politicians, including members of the Grant administration. This is the first of many scandals which will taint Grant's presidency.
• Grant defeats Horace Greeley and is reelected to a second term as president.
• National Woman Suffrage Association vice president Susan B. Anthony insists on casting a ballot in the presidential election. A New York court fines her $100.

March 3, 1873 Congress votes itself a 50 percent pay raise and doubles the salaries of the President and Supreme Court justices. The law, popularly known as the "salary grab," is repealed in 1874, except for the president and the justices' salaries.

1875 The "Whiskey Ring" scandal surfaces. Midwestern distillers are found to be evading federal taxes with the help of government officials, including President Grant's secretary, Orville Babcock.

1876 Yet another scandal rocks the Grant administration as Secretary of War William Belknap is accused of selling trading rights on Indian reservations and army posts.
• As one of his last acts as president, Grant opens the Centennial

THE AMERICAN SCENE

1872 Former Union officers found the National Rifle Association to promote marksmanship among the nation's military and civilian populations.

June The Freedmen's Bureau is closed by Congress because resistance from Southern whites has reduced its effectiveness.
• Congress creates Yellowstone Park in Wyoming to help conserve the nation's endangered resources.
• Congress adopts the Amnesty Act, restoring Southerners' right to hold elective office.

1873 The Panic of 1873 brings the post-Civil War economic boom to a halt. About 5,000 business fail before the end of the year. The resulting nationwide depression will last until 1879.
• Gold becomes the U.S. monetary

Yellowstone National Park

standard after Congress passes the Fourth Coinage Act and eliminates all silver currency. 500,000 immigrants arrive in the U.S.
• Illinois farmer Joseph Glidden begins selling his new invention—barbed wire. By the end of the decade, barbed-wire fences stretch across the West, ending the era of cattle drives and open-range ranching.

Cartoon showing Grant besieged by scandals

Exposition in Philadelphia. The exposition, which celebrates the United States' one-hundredth birthday, features the products of America's farms, factories, and shops.

• Although Grant himself is innocent of wrongdoing, the scandals involving members of his administration taint his image and his bid for a nomination for a third presidential term fails. The Republicans nominate Rutherford B. Hayes instead.

• Democrat Samuel J. Tilden defeats Hayes in the popular vote in the election of 1876. The Republicans dispute the results in the Electoral College, and a special commission is set up to determine the winner.

1877 Democrats agree to accept Hayes as the nineteenth president of the United States in exchange for a Republican pledge to remove the last troops from the former Confederacy, cease enforcing federal Reconstruction policies, and include Southern Democrats in the Hayes administration.

April 14 President Hayes orders the remaining federal troops in Louisiana to leave the state, ending Reconstruction.

1878 Rutherford B. Hayes becomes the first president to use Alexander Graham Bell's invention—the telephone—in the White House.

November 8 Spanish authorities seize the American ship *Virginius* at Havana, Cuba. Because the ship is carrying arms to Cuban rebels, the Spanish execute thirteen American crewmen. The Spanish government later apologizes for the incident, which nearly leads to war between the United States and Spain.

November 18, 1874 The Woman's Christian Temperance Union is founded in Cleveland, Ohio. The organization is part of a growing movement to ban the sale of alcohol.

1875 After a gold strike, prospectors rush into the Black Hills of the Dakota Territory, a region promised to the Sioux Indians by the Treaty of Fort Laramie. War over the Black Hills breaks out the following year.

• Congress passes the Civil Rights Act of 1875. The act, which bars racial discrimination in public places, is overturned by the Supreme Court in 1883.

October 30 Mary Baker Eddy publishes *Science and Health with Key to the Scriptures*. The book inspires the Christian Science movement.

1876 *The Adventures of Tom Sawyer*, by Mark Twain, is published.

• The National League of Baseball is organized. Boston beats Philadelphia, six to five, in the League's first official game.

June 25 Sioux and Cheyenne warriors led by Sitting Bull and Crazy Horse defeat General George Custer's 7th Cavalry at the Little Bighorn River in the Montana Territory. Custer and his 264-man command are killed.

Part I
The Civil War

A Union cavalryman is pictured in this cigarette card, one of a series included as premiums in packets of Duke cigarettes in the late nineteenth century. Abraham Lincoln's presidency spanned the Civil War, almost from the first to the last shots of the conflict. Lincoln took office a few weeks before the Confederate attack on Fort Sumter, and he was assassinated less than a week after General Robert E. Lee's surrender at Appomattox Court House.

Few leaders have faced the challenges that confronted Abraham Lincoln when he took office as president on March 4, 1861. The nation had split in two, and within six weeks of his inauguration the Union and the Confederacy were at war. For four long and bloody years, through times when it seemed that the division between North and South would last, Lincoln provided the leadership that brought the Union victory. Perhaps more important, Lincoln made real the Declaration of Independence's promise that "all men are created equal," by overseeing the end of slavery.

Today, historians place Lincoln with Washington as one of the nation's greatest presidents. During his presidency, however, some people accused Lincoln of acting more like a dictator than a democratic leader. His critics claimed that many of his wartime actions, such as suspending civil rights in parts of the country, exceeded the president's constitutional powers. In one of the few free elections ever held by a nation in the midst of a civil war, Northern voters showed their confidence in Lincoln's leadership by electing him to a second term.

Lincoln might have proved as great a president in peace as in war, but an assassin's bullet deprived him of the chance. Lincoln's tragic death also robbed the nation of the one leader who could have brought North and South back together in a spirit of peace and justice.

ABRAHAM LINCOLN

Abraham Lincoln was born on February 12, 1809, near the town of Hodgenville in Hardin County, Kentucky. His parents, Thomas Lincoln and Nancy Lincoln, were both from Virginia families that had moved west with the frontier. After Abraham's birth, the family moved to Knob Creek, Kentucky. In 1816, Lincoln's father became tangled in a legal battle over land ownership, so the Lincolns moved again, this time to Little Pigeon Creek, Indiana. Less than a year later, Nancy Lincoln died from an epidemic that swept the Indiana frontier. In 1819, Tom Lincoln married a widow, Sarah Johnston. Abraham and his sister, Sarah, came to love their stepmother.

Lincoln grew into a tall, thin, but strong young man with a keen sense of humor. Although he had only a year's worth of formal education, he loved to read. Lincoln often carried a book with him as he worked on his family's and neighbors' farms or did odd jobs around the countryside. At age nineteen, Lincoln and a friend took a boatload of farm goods down the Ohio and Mississippi rivers to New Orleans.

In 1830, the Lincolns moved yet again, this time to Macon County, Illinois. In 1831, Lincoln, now twenty-two, struck out on his own. After another trip to New Orleans, he settled in the small settlement of New Salem, Illinois.

Abraham Lincoln's love of reading began in his boyhood and continued throughout his life. The Bible, Aesop's fables, Shakespeare's plays, and the poetry of Robert Burns were among his favorite works. The influence of Lincoln's wide reading and mastery of the English language shows in his many great speeches. John Hay, who served as Lincoln's secretary during his presidency, wrote that "nothing would have more amazed [Lincoln] while he lived than to hear himself called a man of letters; but this age has produced few greater writers." This painting (above) by Eastman Johnson shows young Lincoln reading by firelight.

The first president from outside the original thirteen states, Abraham Lincoln was born in this log cabin (below) on his father's 350-acre Kentucky farm. Kentucky became a state in 1792, just a decade after Lincoln's grandfather moved there from Virginia. The cabin still exists, housed within a granite building near its original site. Jefferson Davis, future president of the Confederacy, was also born in a log cabin in Kentucky, not far from Lincoln's birthplace.

LINCOLN IN ILLINOIS

New Salem would be Lincoln's home for the next six years. He found work as a clerk in a grocery store and continued to read every chance he got, sometimes walking several miles to borrow a book. In 1832, Lincoln volunteered to serve in the Illinois militia during the Black Hawk War, a conflict between U.S. troops and warriors from the Sauk and Fox Indian tribes. Lincoln saw no fighting in his three months' service, but his fellow volunteers elected him captain of their company.

A growing interest in law and politics led Lincoln to run for a seat in the Illinois legislature. After he lost the election, Lincoln became a partner in a store that soon went bankrupt, leaving him heavily in debt. Determined to pay back his creditors, Lincoln became New Salem's postmaster. The position didn't pay much, but it gave him time to work at part-time jobs such as splitting fence rails and surveying land.

Lincoln ran for the state legislature again in 1834, on the Whig ticket. (The Whigs and Democrats were the two major political parties of the era.) By now, his reputation for intelligence and honesty had spread beyond New Salem, and he won the election. Moving to the state capital, Vandalia, Lincoln began studying law between legislative sessions. He was admitted to the bar in 1836. Three years later the legislature moved to Springfield, the new state capital. Lincoln opened a law office over Springfield Courthouse with his partner, John T. Stuart.

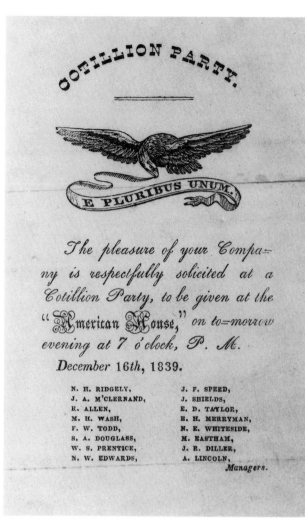

Lincoln helped organize and attend the Christmas cotillion party described in this announcement (above) in December, 1839, the year the Illinois capital moved from Vandalia to Springfield. Stephen A. Douglas, an Illinois politican and lawyer who would later compete with Lincoln for a seat in the United States Senate, is also listed among the invited guests.

This lithograph (below) depicts the Battle of Bad Axe, the last fight of a one-sided war against Sauk and Fox Indians in Illinois and Wisconsin. Lincoln, who served as both a captain and a private in the Sangamon County Rifles, later joked that while he hadn't done any fighting, "I had a good many bloody struggles with the mosquitoes; and I was often hungry."

FAMILY LIFE
AND CAREER

Lincoln's Springfield law office usually handled small legal matters such as wills and deeds, but Lincoln and Stuart once won acquittal for a client in a sensational murder trial. The trial pitted Lincoln against another young Illinois lawyer, Stephen Douglas, who would one day be Lincoln's greatest political rival.

In 1840, Lincoln met Mary Todd, the lively twenty-two-year-old daughter of a prosperous Kentucky businessman. After a brief courtship, the two decided to get married. But then Lincoln had second thoughts. Keenly aware of his modest origins and frontier background, Lincoln felt he wouldn't be a proper husband for Mary. Reluctantly, he broke off the engagement.

Lincoln was soon so depressed that he described himself as "the most miserable man now living." Lincoln and Mary renewed their engagement and were married on November 4, 1842.

Marriage was a source of both joy and anxiety to Lincoln. He loved Mary deeply, but her high-strung, moody nature was sometimes difficult to bear. Lincoln himself could be difficult: He was prone to periods of depression, and his rough frontier humor sometimes offended people. Still, the two were devoted to each other and to their four sons: Robert (born 1843), Edward (born 1846), William (born 1850), and Thomas (born 1853).

Mary Todd Lincoln's life was filled with tragedy and controversy. During the Civil War, some Northern politicians suspected her of disloyalty because of her Southern heritage and the fact that several of her relatives fought for the Confederacy. Others—including her husband—criticized her for spending too much money on White House decorations. The strains of the war years and the assassination of her husband took a heavy toll on Mary: In 1875, she spent a short time in a mental hospital. Mary died in Springfield at the age of sixty-three on July 16, 1882.

A year and a half after his marriage to Mary Todd, Lincoln paid $1,500 for this frame house (right) in Springfield. It was a big change from the rough-hewn log cabins in which the future president had spent his boyhood. The property also included a barn where the Lincolns kept a cow to provide milk for their growing family.

This lithograph (above), published by Currier & Ives in 1867, shows the Lincoln family toward the end of the Civil War. By 1863, the Lincolns had lost two of their four sons to disease: Edward died in 1850, just short of four years old, and William (Willie) at age eleven, in 1862. Thomas (Tad), shown reading with his father, died of illness in 1871. Robert Lincoln is depicted in the uniform of a Union officer. Although he wanted to join the army, Mary Lincoln forbade him to enlist until late in the conflict, when he served on General Ulysses S. Grant's staff.

LINCOLN AND THE REPUBLICAN PARTY

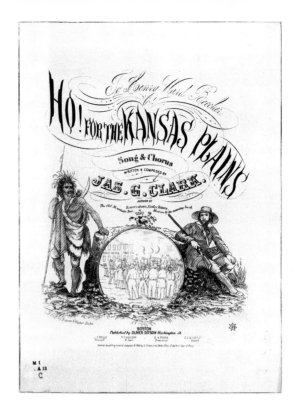

After his marriage, Lincoln continued to serve in the Illinois legislature while his reputation as a skillful lawyer grew. Soon he was arguing cases for powerful clients like the Illinois Central Railroad.

In 1846, Lincoln made his first venture into national politics as a Whig candidate for the House of Representatives. Although Illinois was a mostly Democratic state, Lincoln won. Leaving Mary and their sons in Springfield, he arrived in Washington early in 1847.

Lincoln was a hardworking congressman, but the only attention he attracted came because of his opposition to the Mexican War. He believed that slavery was wrong, and he felt the war's purpose was to gain more land for slavery. (Like most Whigs, Lincoln thought slavery should be allowed to exist in the South but should not spread to any new territories won from Mexico.) Discouraged by President Polk's policies, Lincoln didn't run for reelection in 1848. When his term ended he returned to Springfield and his law office.

In 1855, Lincoln lost an election for the U.S. Senate. Although he remained interested in politics, he concentrated on his law practice in the next few years. But events soon brought him back onto the national scene.

The passage of the Kansas-Nebraska Act in 1854 led to the founding of the Republican Party and marked a turning point in Lincoln's political career. The law organized the Kansas Territory and left the decision of whether to allow slavery to the territory's citizens. Thus, pro- and antislavery settlers rushed into Kansas, each side hoping to win a majority in the elections for a territorial government. This sheet-music cover (above) is to a song written to convince antislavery New Englanders to move to the new territory.

Former army officer John C. Frémont (opposite, top), Republican presidential candidate in the election of 1856, was nicknamed "the Pathfinder" because he had led exploring expeditions to the Far West. Although Frémont opposed slavery, many Republicans distrusted him because of his ambitious personality and his controversial actions during the Mexican War. Ulysses S. Grant, a future Republican president who had fought in the Mexican War, once said that he voted for James Buchanan in 1856 "because I knew Frémont."

This daguerreotype (right), probably taken in Springfield in either 1846 or 1848, is the first known photograph of Abraham Lincoln. It shows him as he looked during his single term in the House of Representatives. In Congress, Lincoln's opposition to slavery grew stronger. He tried to introduce a law to end slavery gradually in Washington, D.C. There was little support for his measure from his own party, the Whigs, and almost none among the Democrats, so the bill was never voted on.

THE LINCOLN-DOUGLAS DEBATES

A new political group, the Republican Party, formed to fight the spread of slavery. The new party attracted many antislavery politicians—including Lincoln. In 1856, Lincoln narrowly lost a bid to become the running mate of John C. Frémont, the Republicans' first presidential candidate.

In 1858, Lincoln decided to run for the Senate against Democrat Stephen Douglas. The two candidates agreed to face off in a series of debates throughout Illinois. With the North and South rapidly moving apart over slavery, the contest between tall, lean Lincoln and short, plump Douglas caught the nation's attention as a symbol of growing national division.

In the debates, Douglas defended his doctrine of "popular sovereignty"—the idea that the citizens of each territory should decide whether to permit slavery. Lincoln, arguing that "a house divided against itself cannot stand," maintained that slavery was morally wrong and should face "ultimate extinction."

Although many observers felt Lincoln was the winner in the debates, Douglas won the election. Nevertheless, the debates made Lincoln one of the best-known Republicans in the country.

Nicknamed "the Little Giant," Stephen Douglas (1813–61; above) didn't let his short stature stand in the way of his political ambitions. A native New Yorker, Douglas moved to Illinois in 1833 and became a lawyer, moving in the same legal and political circles as Abraham Lincoln. But while Lincoln joined the Republican Party and opposed the spread of slavery, Douglas, a Democrat, supported measures that favored slavery and the South—including the Kansas-Nebraska Act, which he sponsored. When the Civil War broke out, however, Douglas pledged his support to his old rival Abraham Lincoln.

This print (below) depicts Lincoln, with Stephen Douglas standing behind him, addressing the audience during one of the debates. The debates attracted huge numbers of people. At the debate at Freeport, a crowd of 15,000 turned out to see the two politicians defend their positions. When Lincoln narrowly lost the Senate race to Douglas, he said that he felt like "the boy who stubbed his toe; I am too big to cry and too badly hurt to laugh."

THE ELECTION OF 1860

Lincoln's national reputation grew after a speaking tour of the Eastern states in 1860. In May of that year, the leading Republicans met in Chicago to pick their candidate for the presidential election. Although Lincoln stayed in Springfield during the convention, his political allies gathered up enough support to have him nominated on the third ballot. In little more than a decade, Abraham Lincoln had gone from an undistinguished Illinois representative to a presidential candidate.

Lincoln faced a disorganized opposition. Slavery split the Democratic Party just as it did the country. Southern Democrats broke off from the party to nominate Vice President John C. Breckinridge of Kentucky. The remaining Democrats chose Stephen Douglas. Supporters of a compromise on slavery organized the Constitutional Union Party, with Senator John Bell of Tennessee as their nominee.

On November 6, with the vote split four ways, Abraham Lincoln emerged as the victor. Lincoln won a majority in the Electoral College, although he received only about 40 percent of the popular vote.

Lincoln's election was an outrage to many Southerners. In December, a state convention in South Carolina voted to secede from the Union. Six other Southern states followed in the next few weeks. Abraham Lincoln would take over leadership of a divided nation on the edge of civil war.

This lithograph (above) from the campaign of 1860 is one of the last portraits showing a clean-shaven Abraham Lincoln. Two weeks before the election, Lincoln received a letter from Grace Bedell, an eleven-year-old girl in Westfield, New York. She urged Lincoln to grow a beard, writing him, "You would look a great deal better for your face is so thin."

During the campaign of 1860, Lincoln's supporters formed "Wide-Awake" clubs and held huge torchlight parades to promote their candidate. Besides torches and banners, the marchers sometimes carried fence rails to celebrate Lincoln's early years as a rail splitter. This engraving (opposite, top), from the October 13, 1860, edition of Harper's Weekly, *shows a "Grand procession of Wide-Awakes" in New York City.*

Lincoln chose not to attend the Republican Convention in Chicago, telling a friend, "I am a little too much a candidate to stay home, and not quite enough a candidate to go." He also did little active campaigning for the presidency. His Democratic rival, Stephen Douglas, campaigned across the country—the first nationwide tour by a presidential candidate. This cartoon (right) shows Douglas "taking the stump," a pun on the frontier practice of making political speeches from atop a tree stump. Lincoln is standing at the far right

LINCOLN GOES TO WASHINGTON

While the Confederacy organized in Montgomery, Alabama, Abraham Lincoln and his family left Springfield for the journey to Washington.

Because there was so much support for the Confederacy in and around Washington, many feared Lincoln wouldn't make it to the capital alive. Alan Pinkerton, a famous detective, persuaded Lincoln that Confederate plotters planned to assassinate him in Baltimore, so the presidential train steamed through the city at night.

The president-elect's secret arrival in Washington didn't inspire much confidence in the people of the North, who nervously wondered how Lincoln would handle the challenge from the South. At his inauguration on the blustery day of March 4, 1861, Lincoln told the crowd that he hoped "the mystic chords of memory" that bound the nation together would keep the crisis from turning into war. But Lincoln warned the South that he would not tolerate secession.

On his first morning as president, Lincoln discovered that he had inherited a touchy situation from former president James Buchanan. As the Southern states seceded, they would seize federal forts and arsenals. But one garrison—Fort Sumter in the harbor at Charleston, South Carolina—remained in federal hands. The new president's advisers urged him to evacuate the troops holding the fort. Lincoln disagreed. Fort Sumter would be defended.

Abraham Lincoln didn't even meet his running mate, Hannibal Hamlin (1809–91; above), until after the Republican Convention in 1860. An outspoken foe of slavery, Hamlin served in the House and Senate as a Democrat from Maine before breaking with the party in 1856 over slavery. As Lincoln's vice president, Hamlin often disagreed with the president's cautious approach to emancipation for the slaves, and he was not renominated in 1864.

The massive dome of the Capitol remained unfinished when Lincoln took office, as this 1861 photograph (right) shows. Washington in 1861 was still very much a Southern city, and pro-Southern feeling ran high in the capital and the surrounding area. During Lincoln's swearing-in ceremony on March 4, army sharpshooters were stationed on rooftops around the Capitol, while cavalry patrolled the city's streets.

This cartoon (below), published just a week after Lincoln's inauguration, portrays the new president as a schoolmaster trying to control a class of unruly boys—in this case, the Southern states. To the South, however, Lincoln's election was no laughing matter. After the election, an editorial in a Georgia newspaper, referring to the street on which the Capitol is located, stated that "whether Pennsylvania Avenue is paved . . . with mangled bodies, the South will never submit to the inauguration of Abraham Lincoln."

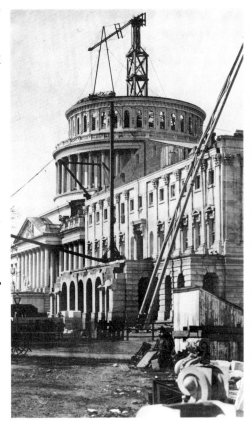

THE STORM BREAKS

On April 11, 1861, South Carolina authorities called on Fort Sumter's commander, Major Robert Anderson, to surrender. When he refused, Confederate artillery began pounding the fort. On April 14, with his men out of water and ammunition, Anderson ordered the American flag hauled down. The Civil War had begun.

Lincoln reacted quickly and decisively to the news of the fort's bombardment. Because Congress wasn't in session, the president used his executive authority to issue several proclamations. One called for a naval blockade of the Confederate states. Another authorized the Northern states to provide 75,000 volunteer troops to put down the "rebellion."

Troops were desperately needed. Washington, the capital of the Union (as the nonseceded states were now called), was surrounded by Confederate Virginia, where Richmond, the capital of the Confederacy, was located, and Maryland, where pro-Confederate feeling ran high. Lincoln could see Virginia's Confederate flags from the White House. The Union responded to Lincoln's call, and soon thousands of soldiers arrived in Washington. These young men were high-spirited, but untrained and undisciplined. It would take time to turn them into an effective army. Lincoln, however, was under pressure from the Northern public and press to make a military move against the Confederacy. In July 1861, the president ordered 35,000 troops under General Irvin McDowell to advance on Richmond.

This cartoon (opposite, top) shows prominent Republican politicians and journalists aboard a sinking boat steered by the new president. The politicians are throwing William Seward over the side. He was a former governor of New York and one of the first prominent politicians to join the Republican Party. Seward, Lincoln's rival for the Republican nomination in 1860 and later Lincoln's secretary of state, used the phrase "Irrepressible Conflict" to describe the growing national split over slavery. The cartoon uses language of the time that would today be considered racist.

Federal troops fire back at their attackers in this Currier & Ives lithograph (right) of the interior of Fort Sumter. Although Confederate gunners poured more than 4,000 shells into the fort during the siege, the defenders suffered only one casualty—a private killed in an accident after the fort had surrendered. The American flag would not fly over Fort Sumter again until its capture by Union forces in February 1865.

JEFFERSON DAVIS: PRESIDENT OF THE CONFEDERACY

In February 1861, representatives from the seceded states met in Montgomery, Alabama, and formally joined as the Confederate States of America. The Confederacy eventually included eleven Southern states, and made Richmond, Virginia, its capital.

The delegates to the Montgomery convention chose former Mississippi senator Jefferson Davis as president. Until the Confederacy's defeat four years later, Davis served as "president" of 9 million Americans.

Davis was born in rural Kentucky in 1808, but the family moved to Mississippi when he was a young boy. After graduating from West Point in 1828, Davis served as an army officer on the frontier and in the Mexican War. In 1835, he married Sarah Taylor, daughter of future president Zachary Taylor, but she died three months after the marriage. Ten years later Davis married Varina Howell.

Davis's four-year presidency was stormy. Besides leading the Confederacy in a war that it was to lose, Davis faced opposition within the Confederate government and among the Southern people. After Richmond fell to Union troops in April 1865, he fled to Georgia, where he was captured. He was imprisoned for two years in Fort Monroe, Virginia. Released in 1867, he spent the rest of his life at his Mississippi home, writing his memoirs.

This Northern cartoon (above) uses an optical illusion to mock Jefferson Davis. Viewed head-on, it depicts a fierce-looking Davis "going to war." Viewed upside down, it shows the Confederate president as a grass-chomping mule "returning from war."

Jefferson Davis wanted the struggle against the Union to continue, even after the fall of Richmond in April 1865. With his wife and a handful of Confederate officials, Davis made his way into Georgia, hoping to reach the West, where some Confederate troops were still fighting. A Union cavalry patrol caught up with the fleeing president on May 10. Davis was taken prisoner while wearing his wife's shawl, but a rumor quickly spread that he had been captured while disguised in women's clothing, as shown in this Northern cartoon (right).

Jefferson Davis (right) thought of himself as a soldier, not a politician, and he had hoped for a general's commission in the Confederate Army. Instead, to his surprise, he received a letter notifying him of his election as president of the Confederacy. Davis reluctantly accepted the post. After the Civil War, Davis was imprisoned for two years in Fort Monroe, Virginia, before his release on bail. After that, he settled in his Mississippi home, Beauvoir, where he wrote his memoirs, The Rise and Fall of the Confederate States. After Davis's death in 1889 at the age of eighty-one, his body was sent to Richmond for burial.

LINCOLN AND THE PROBLEM OF COMMAND

On July 21, McDowell attacked a Confederate force near Manassas, Virginia, along a stream called Bull Run. While the battle raged, Lincoln sat in the White House reading telegrams from the battlefield. They told of a Union victory. They were wrong. The next day, Union soldiers staggered into Washington, weary and discouraged. The first major battle of the war had ended in defeat for the Union.

Bull Run ended Union hopes for a quick victory. For most of the next three years, Lincoln would search for a commander who could defeat the Confederacy. In the meantime, the president realized that he would have to set Union strategy himself. Painfully aware of his lack of military experience, Lincoln studied military textbooks from the Library of Congress in an effort to understand the art of war.

Lincoln soon found able generals to fight in the Western Theater of the war, the area between the Appalachian Mountains and the Mississippi River. Both Ulysses S. Grant and William Tecumseh Sherman quickly began to win territory back from the Confederacy. In Virginia and Maryland, however, the story was different. Lincoln appointed a series of generals to command the Army of the Potomac, the major Union force in the East. But until the spring of 1864, none could adequately meet the challenges presented by such masterful Confederate commanders as Robert E. Lee and Thomas J. "Stonewall" Jackson.

This lithograph (above) shows the First Battle of Bull Run (a second battle was fought near the same site in August 1862). The Union loss convinced Lincoln that defeating the Confederacy would be a long and difficult task. One day after the battle, the president called for the enlistment of 500,000 volunteers for three years of service. Eventually, Congress would take the controversial step of authorizing conscription (the draft) to keep the Union ranks filled.

The Army of the Potomac had gone through several unsuccessful generals by early 1863, when President Lincoln appointed General Joseph Hooker (shown left reviewing troops with Lincoln) as its commander. During Lincoln's visit to Hooker's headquarters, the general bragged that he would soon capture Richmond. In fact, Hooker's campaign to take the Confederate capital ended in a disastrous Union defeat at Chancellorsville in May 1863.

The greatest Union victory in the early years of the war came in April 1862, when New Orleans—the Confederacy's biggest city and busiest port—surrendered to a fleet commanded by Flag Officer David Glasgow Farragut. Farragut's ships reached the city only after a daring dash past the guns of the Confederate forts guarding the mouth of the Mississippi River—the action shown in this lithograph (above). Although the fall of New Orleans sealed off the lower end of the Mississippi, the Union didn't gain control of the entire river until the fall of Vicksburg, Mississippi, more than a year later.

Horace Greeley (left) was the editor of the New York Tribune, the North's most important newspaper. He had called for a Union advance on Richmond in the summer of 1861, but he changed his stance in the aftermath of the defeat at Bull Run. In a letter to the president written a week after the battle, Greeley said that "if it is best for the country and for mankind that we make peace with the rebels, and on their own terms, do not shrink even from that."

When the Civil War began, the general in chief of the U.S. Army was Winfield Scott. Too old and sick for the job, however, Scott resigned in November 1861. Lincoln replaced him with George McClellan, but the young general proved overcautious and slow. Lincoln once wrote to McClellan: "Dear General, if you do not want to use the army I would like to borrow it for a few days." Lincoln finally fired McClellan in December 1862. In 1864, McClellan, a Democrat, challenged Lincoln for the presidency. This Republican cartoon (below) pokes fun at the former Union-commander-turned-presidential-candidate. It shows George McClellan sitting on a gunboat on the James River, where he retreated after the disastrous Peninsular Campaign in 1862.

THE LINCOLN
WHITE HOUSE

Abraham Lincoln is remembered as a
great leader, but during his presidency
many Northerners disliked his personality and disagreed with his policies.
He made some unpopular decisions
during wartime—notably suspending
the right of habeus corpus (a protection against illegal imprisonment in
criminal trials) after the war began.
Lincoln's main challenge was to keep
the Northern government united in its
struggle to defeat the Confederacy.
Some Republicans in Congress urged
him to make the end of slavery a goal
of the Union war effort. But many
Democrats argued that the war should
be limited to restoring the Union.

The president's cabinet was a source
of trouble, too. Secretary of State
William Seward and Treasury Secretary Salmon Chase were ambitious
politicians whose actions often went
against Lincoln's wishes. And even in
the midst of a civil war, the president
had to deal with the day-to-day details
of government—such as facing the
hordes of people who came to the
White House seeking government jobs.

Lincoln also suffered personal
tragedy. In February 1862, the Lincolns' eleven-year-old son, Willie,
became sick and died. Willie's death
plunged the president into a deep
depression and pushed Mary Lincoln
to the edge of madness.

Lincoln found some relief in humor.
He loved to tell jokes and often began
cabinet meetings by reading a humor-
ous story aloud. "If I couldn't tell these
stories," Lincoln told a congressman, "I
would die."

*Robert (above), shown here as a college stu-
dent, was the only one of Lincoln's sons to
live to adulthood. He had the tragic distinc-
tion of being at the scene of three presidential assassinations. Robert watched his own
father die from John Wilkes Booth's bullet in
April 1865. Sixteen years later, Robert, then
secretary of war, walked into Washington's
railroad station during the shooting of President James Garfield. And on September 6,
1901, Robert arrived at the Pan-American
Exposition in Buffalo, New York, moments
after an assassin's bullet struck down President William McKinley.*

*This lithograph (below) shows Lincoln with
his cabinet. Keeping the cabinet united was
one of Lincoln's greatest challenges as president. It included three men who had challenged him for the Republican nomination in
1860, and others (such as Simon Cameron,
Lincoln's first secretary of war) who got
their jobs through political influence, not
experience or ability. Although his relation-
ship with the cabinet was rocky at first, Lincoln soon earned their trust and respect:
Secretary of State Seward described Lincoln
as "the best of us all."*

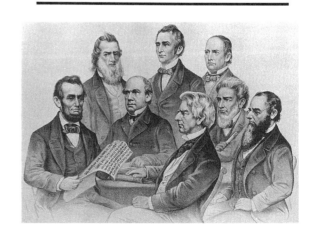

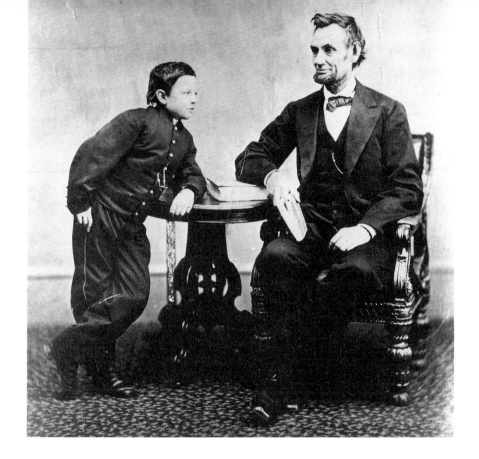

Lincoln took great pleasure in the company of his son Thomas, nicknamed Tad. In this photo (above), Tad is about twelve. During the war years, Tad suffered several bouts of fever, worrying his parents, who had already lost two sons. When Confederate general Robert E. Lee surrendered in April 1865, Lincoln asked the War Department for a sword to give to Tad. Waving his present to the cheers of a joyful crowd, Tad led a parade up Pennsylvania Avenue.

"I feel worried about Mary," Lincoln told a relative during the Civil War. "Her nerves have gone to pieces . . . the strain she has been under has been too much for her mental as well as her physical health." Much of the strain resulted from nasty rumors that Mary was spying for the Confederacy from within the White House. Angered by the accusations, Lincoln appeared before a congressional committee to testify, "I, of my own knowledge, know that it is untrue that any of my family hold treasonable relations with the enemy." This photograph (right) shows Mary in mourning dress, probably following the death of Willie in 1862.

THE EMANCIPATION PROCLAMATION

Although slavery was the chief cause of the Civil War, many Northerners believed that reuniting the country, not freeing the slaves, should be the Union's goal. At first, Lincoln also held this view. In a letter to a newspaper, Lincoln wrote, "My paramount object is to save the Union and is not either to save or destroy slavery."

By the middle of 1862, the president's attitude had changed. He had come to see that slavery was a source of economic strength to the Confederacy. Thus, to defeat the South, slavery had to be destroyed. In the summer of 1862, Lincoln told his cabinet that he planned to proclaim slaves in the Confederate states free if the states didn't return to the Union by January 1, 1863. Secretary of State Seward urged Lincoln to delay the proclamation until Union forces had won an important victory.

In September 1862, Union forces halted a Southern invasion of Maryland in the Battle of Antietam. One day after the battle, Lincoln signed the Emancipation Proclamation, saying, "If my name ever goes down in history, it will be for this act."

The Proclamation did not actually free any slaves, because the Confederacy didn't acknowledge Lincoln's authority. But the document made slavery's end a goal of the Union, and it gave the Northern people a new sense of purpose and determination.

On September 21, 1862, President Lincoln called a cabinet meeting. After reading aloud a story by the humorist Artemus Ward, Lincoln grew serious and said, "I have called you here upon very important business. I have prepared a little paper of much significance . . . I have made a promise to myself—and to my Maker. I am now going to fulfill that promise." With that, Lincoln read the Emancipation Proclamation to the cabinet. Two years later, Francis Bicknell Carpenter recorded the scene in this painting (above).

Some abolitionists and black leaders criticized the Emancipation Proclamation for not going far enough. (For example, the document did not free slaves in the slave states, such as Maryland and Missouri, that stayed in the Union.) But most recognized the Proclamation as the first step toward freedom and equality for black Americans. In gratitude, the black community of Baltimore presented Lincoln with this print (left), which shows the president reading the Bible with Sojourner Truth, a former slave and abolitionist leader.

THE GETTYSBURG ADDRESS

In June 1863, Confederate commander Robert E. Lee led his Army of Northern Virginia into the North. The Army of the Potomac moved to stop them. During the first three days of July, a huge battle raged near the small town of Gettysburg, Pennsylvania. It ended with Lee's defeated army retreating back to Virginia.

In November, Lincoln traveled to Gettysburg to help dedicate a cemetery for some of the more than 3,000 Union soldiers who had died in the battle. After a two-hour speech by Edward Everett, a famous speaker, Lincoln stood up to address the crowd of 20,000 people. The president spoke briefly (only for about three minutes) but movingly of the soldiers' sacrifice. It was up to the people of the North to see the war through to the end, so that the soldiers' deaths would not be in vain, and so "that this nation, under God, shall have a new birth of freedom —and that government of the people, by the people, and for the people, shall not perish from the earth."

Although Lincoln's Gettysburg Address attracted little attention at the time, it is now considered one of the greatest presidential speeches. In a few hundred words, Lincoln had given voice to the deepest feelings of a nation struggling to understand the suffering and sacrifice of a bitter civil war.

When Lincoln finished speaking, there was only a scattering of applause. Sitting down, he remarked to his bodyguard that the speech was a "flat failure." But some recognized Lincoln's achievement. Edward Everett, the former Massachusetts governor who gave the main address at the ceremony, wrote to Lincoln: "I should be glad if I could flatter myself that I came as near the central idea of the occasion, in two hours, as you did in two minutes." This portrait (above) shows Lincoln with his hand resting on a copy of the address.

According to a popular story, Lincoln wrote the Gettysburg Address on an envelope while aboard the train carrying him to the battlefield. In fact, Lincoln carefully composed the short speech in Washington, but he did revise it in Gettysburg. This document (opposite, top) is one of the few surviving drafts of the address in Lincoln's own handwriting. This version differs slightly from the speech the president delivered.

This painting (right) shows one of the most dramatic scenes of the Battle of Gettysburg— the Confederate assault on an important hill called Little Round Top, which was defended by a single Union regiment. The Union troops held off the attackers despite heavy casualties. Gettysburg remains the largest battle ever fought in North America.

Four score and seven years ago our fathers brought forth, upon this continent, a new nation, conceived in Liberty, and dedicated to the proposition that all men are created equal.

Now we are engaged in a great civil war, testing whether that nation, or any nation, so conceived, and so dedicated, can long endure. We are met here on a great battle-field of that war. We have come to dedicate a portion of it, as a final resting place for those who here gave their lives, that that nation might live. It is altogether fitting and proper that we should do this.

But in a larger sense we can not dedicate—we can not consecrate—we can not hallow this ground. The brave men, living and dead, who struggled here, have consecrated it, far above our poor power to add or detract. The world will little note, nor long remember, what we say here, but can never forget what they did here. It is for us, the living, rather to be dedicated here to the unfinished work, which they have, thus far, so nobly carried on. It is rather for us to be here dedicated to the great task remaining before us—that from these honored dead we take increased devotion to that cause for which they here gave the last full measure of devotion—that we here highly resolve that these dead shall not have died in vain; that this nation shall have a new birth of freedom, and that this government of the people, by the people, for the people, shall not perish from the earth.

NEW COMMANDERS, NEW FRUSTRATIONS

Shortly after Gettysburg, news of another Union victory reached the White House: A Union army led by Ulysses S. Grant had captured Vicksburg, Mississippi. The fall of Vicksburg cut the eastern part of the Confederacy off from the West and gave the Union control of the Mississippi River. "The Father of Waters," said Lincoln happily, using the Indian name for the river, "again flows unvexed to the sea."

Despite the victories at Gettysburg and Vicksburg, the Confederacy remained defiant. But Lincoln had finally found the general he'd been looking for since 1861—Ulysses S. Grant. In early 1864, Lincoln ordered Grant east to take charge of all Union military operations.

While Grant took on the task of defeating the Confederacy, Lincoln faced new political challenges. Looking toward peace, Lincoln had proposed what he called the "Ten Percent Plan" for the reconstruction of the Union. Under its terms, a Confederate state could be readmitted to the Union if 10 percent of its voting population swore an oath of loyalty to the United States. This policy was too moderate for some Republicans in Congress. Called the "Radical Republicans," or simply the Radicals, these lawmakers wanted to punish the South with a harsher plan, outlined in the Wade-Davis Bill. Lincoln vetoed the bill, but the conflict between Lincoln and the Radicals continued.

Ulysses S. Grant (above) first met Abraham Lincoln at a White House reception on the evening of March 8, 1864, shortly after the new commander's arrival in Washington. Eager for a glimpse of the famous general, the crowd at the White House demanded that Grant stand up on a sofa so they could get a better look. The attention embarrassed the modest Union commander. "I have had enough of this show business," Grant later told the president.

One of Lincoln's toughest jobs as president was dealing with the "Copperheads"—Northerners, most of them Democrats, who favored a negotiated peace, even if it meant independence for the Confederacy. (The Copperheads got their name from the copper Indian-head pennies they wore on their lapels.) When the leading Copperhead, Clement Vallandigham, was arrested and sentenced to jail, Lincoln converted his sentence to banishment to the Confederacy. The anti-Copperhead song sheet pictured here (right) urges Northerners to fight against the "Home Traitors."

By the end of 1863, the tide of war had turned in the North's favor. The Union's superiority in troops and weapons was beginning to wear down the outnumbered and isolated Confederacy. New developments such as the telegraph allowed President Lincoln to stay in constant contact with armies in the field. And thanks to the North's booming economy, Union forces could count on a steady flow of food and supplies, while Southern soldiers were often on the verge of starvation. This photograph (right) shows a long train of Union supply wagons entering Petersburg, Virginia, near the end of the long campaign to capture Richmond.

THE ELECTION OF 1864

The chief issue of the election of 1864 was the war. The Republicans wanted to see the war end with the South defeated on the battlefield and slavery abolished. Many Democrats wanted to negotiate a peace settlement immediately, even if it meant independence for the Confederacy.

In June, the Republicans met in Baltimore under the name of the National Union Convention to attract Democratic support. They nominated Lincoln for a second term, with Andrew Johnson, a Democrat from Tennessee, as his running mate. The Democrats picked George B. McClellan, a former commander of the Army of the Potomac, to run for president.

As election day drew near, it seemed that Lincoln would lose. The Northern public was weary of war. Both Grant and Sherman were advancing into key Confederate strongholds, but their progress was slow and casualties were often shockingly high. The president himself circulated a note among his cabinet acknowledging his slim chance of reelection. Then, Sherman's army captured Atlanta in September. The victory raised spirits in the North and led many voters to change their minds about Lincoln. The president won reelection by a comfortable margin.

Lincoln faced a challenge from within his own party in 1864. A group of Republicans who opposed a second term for Lincoln formed the Independent Republican Party in a convention at Cleveland, Ohio, in July. This splinter group nominated John C. Frémont for president, with John Cochrane of New York as his running mate. In September, however, Frémont withdrew from the race and threw his support to Lincoln. Shown here (above) is a banner from the short-lived Frémont-Cochrane campaign.

This political cartoon (right) compares the race for the White House to a round of bagatelle, a popular table game of the era. While the Democratic candidates—former Union general George McClellan and his running mate, Ohio congressman George Pendleton—look on, Lincoln promises General Grant and his own running mate, Andrew Johnson, "I'll do the best I can, Andy, I can do no more." Lounging on the right is Copperhead leader Clement Vallandigham, who slipped back into the Union to fight Lincoln's bid for reelection.

During the military and political battles of the Civil War, Lincoln had an advantage over previous presidents—the telegraph. The device allowed him to communicate instantly with both his generals in the field and his political allies in distant parts of the country—such as Governor William Pickering of Oregon Country, who sent this greeting to Lincoln during the election campaign of 1864.

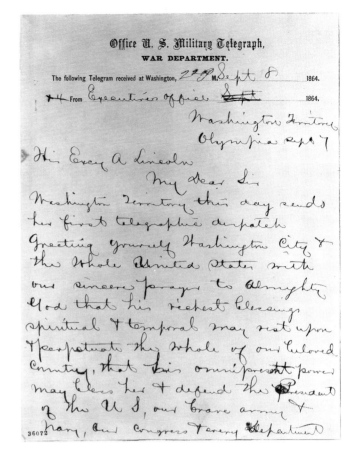

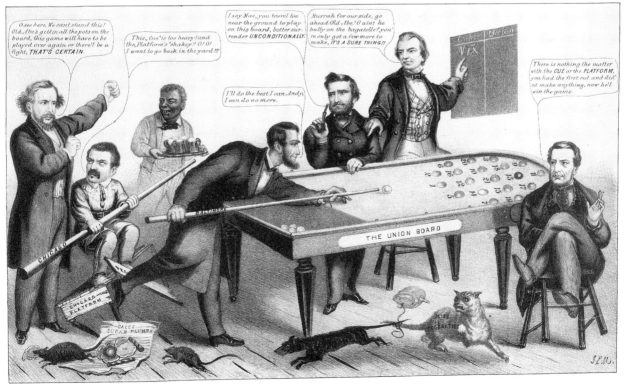

LINCOLN'S SECOND INAUGURATION

By the first months of 1865, Grant's army had surrounded Petersburg, Virginia, only a few miles from Richmond. Sherman's forces had marched from Atlanta to Savannah on the Atlantic Coast, cutting a path of destruction across the South. The Union blockade of Southern ports had cut the Confederacy off from overseas supplies. Hunger, sickness, and desertions made the Confederate armies weaker each day.

The Confederate government, realizing its desperate situation, requested a secret conference to talk over peace terms. On February 3, Lincoln and Secretary of State Seward traveled to Hampton Roads, Virginia, where they met with Confederate vice president Alexander Stephens aboard the steamboat *River Queen*. The conference was a failure. Lincoln refused to make peace on the basis of Southern independence or the continuation of slavery. The war would go on to the end.

On March 4, 1865, Abraham Lincoln was sworn in for a second term as president. In a moving inaugural address, he urged the people of the North not to give in to hatred of the South after the war ended: "With malice toward none, with charity for all, with firmness in the right, as God gives us to see the right, let us continue the work we are in . . . and do all that may achieve a just, and a lasting peace, among ourselves, and with all nations."

This cartoon from Harper's Weekly, *titled "Long Abraham a Little Longer," celebrates Lincoln's election to a second term. Lincoln won with 212 electoral votes (Democrat George McClellan received only 21) and 55 percent of the popular vote. Some observers expected most Union soldiers to vote for McClellan because he had been a popular commander of the Army of the Potomac. The army, however, "went for Old Abe" by a vote of about 117,000 to 34,000. When he received the election results, Lincoln told a crowd of supporters, "It is no pleasure to triumph over anyone, but I give thanks to the Almighty for this evidence of the people's resolution to stand by free government and the rights of humanity."*

BILL OF FARE
OF THE
Presidential Inauguration Ball
IN THE
CITY OF WASHINGTON, D. C.,
On the 6th of March 1865.

Oyster Stews . . . .
Terrapin " . . . .
Oysters, pickled . . . .

BEEF.
Roast Beef . . . .
Filet de Beef . . . .
Beef à-la-mode . . . .
Beef à l'anglais . . . .

VEAL.
Leg of Veal . . . .
Fricandeau . . . .
Veal Malakoff . . . .

POULTRY.
Roast Turkey . . . .
Boned " . . . .
Roast Chicken . . . .
Grouse, boned and roast . . . .

GAME.
Pheasant . . . .
Quail . . . .
Venison . . . .

PATETES.
Patète of Duck en gelée . . . .
Patète de fois gras . . . .

SMOKED.
Ham . . . .
Tongue en gelee . . . .
do plain . . . .

SALADES.
Chicken . . . .
Lobster . . . .

Ornamental Pyramides.
Nougate . . . .
Orange . . . .
Caramel with Fancy Cream Candy .
Cocoanut . . . .
Macaroon . . . .

Croquant . . . .
Chocolate . . . .
Tree Cakes . . . .

CAKES AND TARTS.
Almond Sponge . . . .
Belle Alliance . . . .
Dame Blanche . . . .
Macaroon Tart . . . .
Tart à la Nelson . . . .
Tarte à l'Orleans . . . .
do à la Portugaise . . . .
do à la Vienne . . . .
Pound Cake . . . .
Sponge Cake . . . .
Lady Cake . . . .
Fancy small Cakes . . . .

JELLIES AND CREAMS.
Calf-foot and Wine Jelly . . . . . .
Charlotte à la Russe . . . .
do do Vanilla . . . .
Blanc Mangue . . . .
Crème Neapolitane . . . .
do à la Nelson . . . .
do Chateaubriand . . . .
do à la Smyrna . . . .
do do Nesselrode . . . .
Bombe à la Vanilla . . . .

ICE CREAM.
Vanilla . . . .
Lemon . . . .
White Coffee . . . .
Chocolate . . . .
Burnt Almonds . . . .
Maraschino . . . .

FRUIT ICES.
Strawberry . . . .
Orange . . . .
Lemon . . . .

DESSERT.
Grapes, Almonds, Raisins, &c

Coffee and Chocolate.

Furnished by **G. A. BALZER**, CONFECTIONER,
Cor. 9th & D Sts., Washington, D. C.

On March 6, two days after the swearing-in ceremony, an inaugural ball was held at the White House. This print (above) shows the president and First Lady greeting guests. For the occasion, Mary Lincoln wore a white silk dress that cost more than $2,000—an enormous sum in 1865. Between dances, the partygoers feasted on the items listed on this menu (left).

THE UNION
TRIUMPHANT

On March 23, 1865, President Lincoln left Washington to meet with General Grant in Virginia. Shortly after Lincoln's arrival at Grant's headquarters, Union forces broke through the Confederate lines around Petersburg, opening the way into the Confederate capital. On April 3, the Confederate government fled, and the first Union troops entered Richmond. The next day, Lincoln toured the captured city to the cheers of Union troops and freed slaves.

On April 9, Robert E. Lee surrendered his exhausted Army of Northern Virginia to Grant at Appomattox Court House, in Virginia. Pockets of Southern resistance remained, but the war was essentially over. When news of Lee's surrender reached Washington, a joyous crowd marched to the White House. Lincoln declined the crowd's demand for a speech, but the next day he spoke from his balcony.

It was to be Lincoln's last public speech. In the crowd was a handsome, fiercely pro-Southern actor named John Wilkes Booth. For months Booth and a handful of friends had plotted against the president. Before Lee's surrender, Booth had planned to kidnap the president and hold him hostage to win the release of Confederate prisoners of war. Now, hearing Lincoln voice his approval of a proposal to give some freed slaves the vote, Booth made up his mind to kill the president.

The strain of four years of bitter civil war shows plainly in this photograph of Lincoln (right), one of the last portraits made before his death. The photographer was Mathew Brady, one of the greatest Civil War-era photographers.

President Lincoln was at the Army of the Potomac's base at City Point on the James River when the news of Richmond's fall arrived. "Thank God I have lived to see this," Lincoln told General Horace Porter. "It seems to me that I have been dreaming a horrid dream for four years, and now the nightmare is gone. I want to see Richmond." Escorted by a few sailors, Lincoln and Grant reached the city just hours after its capture. Hundreds of slaves, freed with the arrival of Union troops, gathered joyfully around the president, as this engraving (below) shows.

THE ASSASSINATION OF ABRAHAM LINCOLN

Abraham Lincoln spent the day of April 14, 1865, discussing Reconstruction policies with his cabinet and General Grant. The president told Grant that the night before he had dreamed he was on a ship moving slowly toward a shore hidden in darkness. It was the same dream, Lincoln said, that had disturbed his sleep before many of the key battles and events of the war.

In the evening, Lincoln and his wife went to Ford's Theatre in Washington to see the play *Our American Cousin*. The Lincolns settled into a private booth with their guests, a Union officer and his fiancée. The president's bodyguard slipped away to get a better view of the play, or a drink of water—no one is sure which.

Shortly after ten o'clock, John Wilkes Booth stepped into the president's box. Taking aim with a pistol at the back of the president's head, he fired a single shot. Lincoln slumped forward, a bullet in his brain. Waving a knife, Booth jumped from the box to the stage (breaking his leg in the process) and fled into the night. For a moment there was silence, broken by the screams of Mary Lincoln. A doctor pushed his way through the crowd and into the presidential box. "His wound is mortal," the doctor said after examining Lincoln. "It is impossible for him to recover."

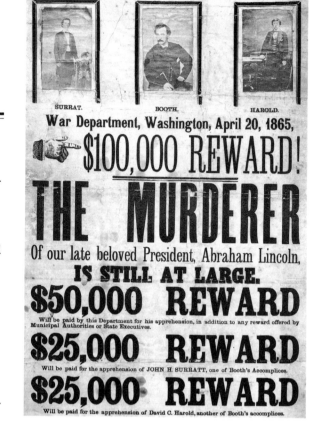

This poster (above) was circulated in and around Washington after Lincoln's death. Although the plot to kill Lincoln and bring down the Union government was solely the work of Booth and his friends, some government officials—including Secretary of War Edwin Stanton—believed Booth had acted on orders from Jefferson Davis.

As shown in this engraving (right), Booth mounted a horse waiting outside Ford's Theatre and escaped across the Potomac River into Maryland. There he was joined by another conspirator, David Herold. After waking up a doctor to set Booth's broken leg, the pair moved deep into the countryside. They were resting in a tobacco barn when a troop of Union cavalry caught up with them on the morning of April 26. Herold surrendered immediately, but Booth refused to leave the barn. After the troops set the barn on fire, Sergeant Boston Corbett shot Booth, mortally wounding him. The assassin died two hours later.

A newspaper artist for Harper's Weekly drew this illustration showing Booth firing at the president's head from close range. Booth then slashed Major Henry Rathbone, one of the Lincolns' guests, with a knife before leaping from the presidential box to the stage.

"NOW HE BELONGS TO THE AGES"

Soldiers carried Abraham Lincoln's unconscious body to a boardinghouse across Tenth Street. As a tearful crowd gathered in the street outside, members of the government arrived to keep watch at the dying president's bedside. Disturbing news arrived: One of Booth's fellow conspirators had stabbed Secretary of State Seward. (Seward survived. And another conspirator, ordered by Booth to kill Vice President Andrew Johnson, failed to carry out the attack.)

At 7:22 on the morning of April 15, the president's breathing stopped. Looking down at Lincoln, Secretary of War Edwin Stanton whispered sadly, "Now he belongs to the ages." Four hours later, as news of Lincoln's assassination spread across a stunned nation, Andrew Johnson was sworn in as president.

On April 19, a funeral procession carried Lincoln's coffin from the White House to the Capitol. Mary Lincoln, hysterical with grief, was unable to attend the funeral ceremonies.

Two days later, a train bearing the bodies of Lincoln and his beloved son Willie left Washington. After a journey through the North to give people an opportunity to say farewell to the murdered president, the train arrived at Springfield, Illinois, on May 4. Abraham Lincoln was home at last.

Booth's fellow conspirators were rounded up quickly in the weeks following the assassination. After trials by a military court, four of the people convicted of taking part in the plot were sentenced to death. Several others received prison sentences. This photograph (above) shows the crowd gathering to watch the hanging of the condemned conspirators on July 7, 1865, in the yard of Washington's Old Penitentiary.

The train bearing Lincoln's body arrived in New York City on April 25. More than 80,000 people watched in silence as the president's coffin was borne through the streets, as depicted in this lithograph (right). In all, several million Americans turned out to mourn the fallen president as the funeral train made its 1,700-mile journey from Washington to Springfield.

In this sentimental print, George Washington welcomes Abraham Lincoln to heaven. It is one of countless popular artworks celebrating the slain president's character and accomplishments. Ironically, Lincoln was far from popular as president; only after his death did people recognize his true greatness.

Part II
Reconstruction

It was in the house pictured on this cigarette card that Robert E. Lee surrendered the Army of Northern Virginia to Ulysses S. Grant on April 9, 1865, ending the Civil War. Grant led the Union armies to victory in the Civil War, but as president during the last part of Reconstruction he failed to heal the division between North and South, and black and white.

In his second inaugural address, in March 1865, Abraham Lincoln described "a just and lasting peace" between North and South. But the two presidents who followed him couldn't make this a reality. Andrew Johnson and Ulysses S. Grant both performed great services for the Union, but their presidencies fell short of their promise. As a result, Reconstruction was a time of bitterness between North and South and a time of conflict and corruption in Washington. The true victims of Reconstruction were the former slaves of the South, who saw their movement toward political equality stall and ultimately stop.

Johnson, a Southerner and a Democrat but a loyal supporter of the Union, took office after Lincoln's assassination. Johnson soon became caught up in a bitter battle with Congress over Reconstruction policy. The battle between president and Congress escalated into impeachment in March 1868. Johnson escaped conviction by one vote, but the conflict crippled his single-term presidency.

Running on the Republican ticket, Ulysses S. Grant won the election of 1868 and was reelected in 1872. Grant's presidency is a story of good intentions and poor judgment. Although Grant was himself an honest man, many of the people he appointed to government posts were not. When Grant left office in 1877, his reputation was badly tarnished by the widespread corruption of his administration.

ANDREW JOHNSON

Andrew Johnson was born on December 29, 1808, in Raleigh, North Carolina. His childhood was one of desperate poverty. Johnson's father, a laborer, died when he was three, and his widowed mother couldn't afford to send Andrew or his brother to school. At the age of thirteen, Johnson was apprenticed to a tailor. He would learn the tailor's trade by serving as an unpaid helper.

Johnson grew skilled with needle and thread and he learned to read from an assistant tailor. But Johnson disliked being an apprentice and soon ran away to South Carolina. Returning to Raleigh, he convinced his mother and her new husband to move west. The family arrived in Greeneville, Tennessee, in 1826, where Johnson set up his own tailor shop.

In 1827, Johnson married Eliza McCardle, the daughter of a local shoemaker. Eliza taught Johnson to write and encouraged his growing interest in politics. At nineteen, Johnson won his first election, as alderman. Despite his lack of a formal education, Johnson gained a reputation as an effective politician and a skilled speaker. In 1834, he was elected mayor of Greeneville.

Like many Tennessee politicians, Johnson was a supporter of Andrew Jackson and the Democratic Party. In 1835, with Jackson in the White House, Johnson won election to the state legislature.

This portrait (above) shows how Eliza McCardle Johnson (1810–76) appeared late in her life. During her time as First Lady, she was too ill to play a prominent role at White House functions. Mrs. Johnson attended only two official events while her husband was president: a visit by the Queen of Hawaii in 1866, and a "children's ball" to celebrate the president's sixtieth birthday in December 1868. Eliza's strong faith in her husband and support for him during his impeachment won her the respect of official Washington.

Andrew Johnson opened this tailor shop (below) shortly after moving to Greeneville, Tennessee, in 1826. When the future president became Greeneville's mayor, the tailor shop also served as town hall. Johnson was proud of his ability as a tailor. As governor of Tennessee, he sewed a suit for the governor of Kentucky; the other governor, a former blacksmith, sent Johnson a handmade shovel and fireplace tongs in return.

JOHNSON AND
THE UNION

Although Johnson failed to win reelection in 1837, he returned to the legislature two years later and also served a term in the state senate. As a Tennessee politician, Johnson attacked the "slavocracy," the wealthy slaveowning planters who held power in the state. Johnson never forgot his humble origins and always believed he represented the common man. Despite his dislike of slaveowners, Johnson wasn't sympathetic toward the slaves themselves. Like many white Americans of the time, he was deeply prejudiced against blacks.

Johnson entered national politics in 1842, winning the first of five terms in the House. He left Congress in the 1850s to serve as governor of Tennessee, but he returned to Washington in 1857 as a senator.

Although Johnson voted for many pro-Southern causes while in the Senate, his loyalty to the Union grew stronger as the Civil War approached. Attacking secession as "hell-born and hell-bound," he stayed in the Senate after Tennessee left the Union—the only senator from a Confederate state to do so. Johnson's courageous stand made him one of the most hated men in the South and a hero in the North. In 1862, after Union forces won control of most of Tennessee, Abraham Lincoln rewarded Johnson's loyalty with an appointment as the state's military governor.

Because of his pro-Union views, Senator Johnson faced angry mobs and death threats in the tense months between Lincoln's election and the attack on Fort Sumter. Once, while he was speaking in a church in Kingsport, Tennessee, a hostile audience tried to shout him down. Johnson took a pistol from his pocket, laid it on the pulpit, and calmly continued his speech. This portrait (opposite, top) shows Johnson as a senator, wearing one of the plain black suits he favored.

This illustration (right) shows Union troops parading in Nashville, Tennessee, a few days after the city's capture in February 1862. With most of western and central Tennessee under Union control, President Lincoln sent Johnson back to the state as its military governor. In September 1862, Eliza Johnson—who had remained in Tennessee after it seceded—received the Confederate government's permission to cross into Union territory to rejoin her husband. The grueling journey left her in poor health for the rest of her life.

ANDREW JOHNSON TAKES OFFICE

As military governor of Tennessee, Andrew Johnson gave amnesty to Confederates who swore loyalty to the Union, and he supported an amendment to the state constitution outlawing slavery.

In the summer of 1864, delegates to the National Union Convention—the Republicans, plus Democrats who supported Lincoln—picked Andrew Johnson as the president's running mate. Lincoln and Johnson, "the rail splitter and the tailor," went on to victory in November.

Johnson's vice presidency didn't begin well. The vice president-elect fell sick a few days before the inauguration, and just before the ceremony he made the mistake of treating his illness with whiskey. When the time came for the vice-presidential inaugural address, Johnson made a "drunken foolish speech," in the words of one senator. The incident deeply embarrassed Johnson, but Lincoln defended him, telling friends, "I have known Andy Johnson for many years. He made a bad slip the other day, but you need not be scared; Andy ain't a drunkard."

On the night of April 14, 1865, Johnson was awakened in his room at the Kirkwood House hotel with the news that Abraham Lincoln had been shot. After visiting the dying president's bedside, Johnson returned to his hotel, where the next morning he was sworn in as president by Chief Justice Salmon Chase.

Portraits of Lincoln and Johnson decorate the "Grand National Union Banner for 1864" (above). The Lincoln-Johnson ticket won the election, but some Northerners attacked the modest background of the two candidates. According to an editorial in a New York newspaper, "the age of statesmen is gone. The age of rail-splitters and tailors . . . has succeeded."

Vice President Johnson stands watch by Abraham Lincoln's deathbed in this Currier & Ives lithograph (opposite, top). Lincoln's assassination and his own sudden succession to the presidency left Johnson stunned. After being sworn in, the new president told Lincoln's cabinet, "I feel incompetent to perform duties so important and responsible as those which have been so unexpectedly thrown upon me."

Salmon P. Chase, Chief Justice of the United States, administered the oath of office to Johnson shortly after Lincoln died on April 15. This wood engraving (right) from Frank Leslie's Illustrated Newspaper *shows the solemn ceremony, which took place in the parlor of the Kirkwood House.*

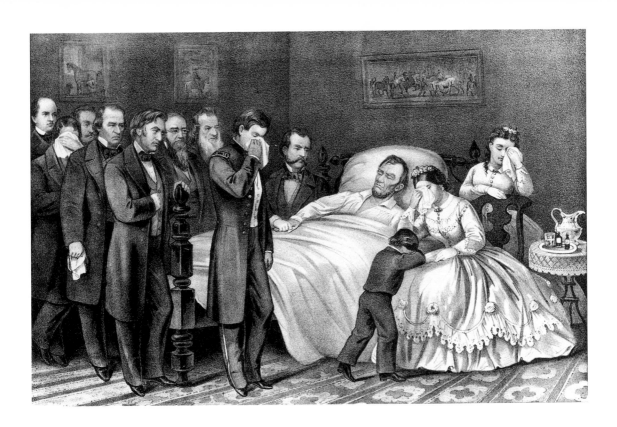

JOHNSON VS. THE RADICALS

At first, the Radical Republicans in Congress were glad that Andrew Johnson would lead the newly reunited nation. They knew Johnson hated the "slavocracy," and they believed he would support their plans for a harsh peace with the South. Lincoln, one leading Radical said, had had "too much of the milk of human kindness." Johnson, on the other hand, appeared only too happy to punish the defeated Confederacy.

The fiercely independent Johnson, however, refused to play the Radicals' game. In May, he announced his Reconstruction plan. It pardoned most ex-Confederates and left the former Confederate states to reconstruct their governments by themselves. This policy angered the Radicals, who wanted Congress to oversee Reconstruction. They believed that only strong, stern Reconstruction policies would safeguard the rights of the newly freed slaves and protect them from vengeful whites. Some Radicals also wanted to give male ex-slaves the vote, knowing that these freedmen would probably vote Republican—thus increasing the Radicals' power in Congress.

In 1866, Johnson vetoed two Radical-sponsored bills, the Civil Rights Act of 1866 (which granted citizenship to former slaves), and a law to provide funding for the Freedmen's Bureau, a federal organization that helped slaves make the transition to freedom. Congress overrode both vetoes. The battle lines were now drawn for one of the worst political fights in presidential history.

This print (right) shows the chamber of the House of Representatives as it looked in 1866, when the Radical Republicans held most of the power in Congress. Hoping to bring more Democrats to Congress and win public approval for his policies, Johnson went on a cross-country speaking tour in the summer of 1866. The tour was a failure, because the hot-tempered Johnson sometimes exchanged insults with angry crowds.

Just before the end of the Civil War, Congress created the Bureau of Refugees, Freedmen, and Abandoned Lands (better known as the Freedmen's Bureau) to aid the reconstruction of the South. One of its tasks, as shown in this newspaper illustration (opposite, bottom), was to protect freed slaves from vengeful whites. The bureau soon became caught in the political fight between Johnson and Congress when the president vetoed a bill to extend the organization's life. Congress managed to override Johnson's veto, but the bureau never had the money or manpower to be truly effective.

The major foreign-policy achievement of Andrew Johnson's administration was the purchase of Alaska from Russia. William Seward, who continued as secretary of state after Lincoln's death, negotiated the deal. The United States paid $7.2 million for a territory of almost 600,000 square miles— or about 2 cents per acre. As this cartoon (below) shows, however, many people believed that buying this land of "polar bears and icebergs" was a foolish move, and they called Alaska "Seward's Folly."

THE IMPEACHMENT OF ANDREW JOHNSON

In early 1867, Congress passed the first of several Reconstruction acts. These laws put the South under military rule and required the ex-Confederate states to ratify the Fourteenth Amendment—which guaranteed citizenship to former slaves—before they could rejoin the Union. Congress also passed the Tenure of Office Act, which prohibited the president from firing a cabinet member without the Senate's approval. Winning control of Reconstruction wasn't enough for the Radicals. They wanted to remove the president from power completely.

Ironically, Johnson himself gave the Radicals their chance. The president considered the Tenure of Office Act unconstitutional, and he decided to put it to the test. In August 1867, Johnson defied the act by firing Secretary of War Edwin Stanton, who had been appointed by Lincoln.

President Johnson hoped the Supreme Court would back him up, but the Court chose not get involved. Instead, the House of Representatives voted to impeach (bring charges of misconduct against) the president in February 1868.

Edwin Stanton (1814–69; above) was at the center of the controversy that led to President Johnson's impeachment. Stanton, a brilliant but stubborn lawyer and politician, had been appointed secretary of war by Abraham Lincoln in 1862. Johnson kept Stanton in his own cabinet until the secretary's pro-Radical views presented too much of a conflict. Stanton finally stepped down after the Radicals failed to force Johnson from office. In 1869, President Ulysses S. Grant appointed Stanton to the Supreme Court, but he died before he could serve.

"Resolved: that Andrew Johnson be impeached of high crimes and misdemeanors." So began the impeachment resolution passed by the House of Representatives on February 24, 1868. The great photographer Mathew Brady took this group portrait (opposite, top) of the House impeachment committee a few days later.

The leader of the move for Johnson's impeachment was Representative Thaddeus Stevens (1792–1868) of Pennsylvania. In this newspaper illustration (right), he is making his final speech in the House of Representatives before bringing the debate to the Senate floor. Stevens, a longtime enemy of slavery, had a burning hatred of the South—perhaps because Confederate troops destroyed a factory he owned during the Gettysburg Campaign in 1863.

TRIAL AND ACQUITTAL

For the first—and so far only—time in American history, a president faced an impeachment trial. The House adopted eleven articles of impeachment against Johnson. Only three of them, including his violation of the Tenure of Office Act, had any real importance. But if convicted by a Senate vote, Johnson could be removed from office. Because Johnson had no vice president, the acting president, or president pro tempore, of the Senate, Radical Republican Benjamin Wade, would become president.

In accordance with the Constitution, the president's trial would be held in the Senate, with Chief Justice Chase as the presiding judge. The trial began on March 13, 1868. Johnson stayed away from the Senate, leaving his defense in the hands of his lawyers. For more than two months the president's lawyers argued with the prosecution, which was led by two fiery Radicals from the House, Benjamin Butler of Massachusetts and Thaddeus Stevens of Pennsylvania.

There were fifty-four senators, most of them Republicans allied with the Radicals. The prosecution needed a two-thirds majority of thirty-six to convict the president. On May 16, the Senate voted on the most serious articles. Before the vote, seven Republican senators who had initially favored conviction changed their minds. The final count included nineteen votes for acquittal—leaving the prosecution one vote short of the two-thirds majority.

So many people wanted to attend the impeachment hearings that the Senate had to print up tickets (above). The lucky few who managed to get into the Senate gallery witnessed a heated legal duel between the president's defense lawyers and the congressional prosecution.

Stevens reads his draft of the impeachment resolution to the Senate in this wood engraving (opposite, top). In failing health by the time the president came to trial, Stevens died shortly after Johnson's acquittal.

This cartoon (right), printed after Johnson's acquittal, shows leading Radical Republicans trying to revive a dead and decaying horse named "impeachment." Johnson received word of his victory with tears of joy. When she heard the news, Eliza Johnson quietly told William Crook, the president's bodyguard, "I knew he would be acquitted. I knew it."

JOHNSON'S LATER YEARS

Andrew Johnson had narrowly won acquittal, but Congress remained dead-set against him. He blasted the legislature in his last speech before leaving office: "Our own history, although embracing a period of less than a century, affords abundant proof that most, if not all, of our domestic troubles are directly traceable to violations of the organic law [the Constitution] and excessive legislation. The most striking illustrations of this fact are . . . the enactments of the last three years upon the question of Reconstruction."

Johnson had hoped that his old party would nominate him for reelection in 1868, but the Democrats instead chose former New York governor Horatio Seymour. In March 1869, Johnson handed over the White House to the victor, Republican Ulysses S. Grant, and returned to Tennessee.

Despite the battles of his presidency, Johnson kept his appetite for politics. He ran for Congress as a Democrat in 1869 and 1872, both times unsuccessfully. In 1874, when the controversies of Reconstruction were beginning to cool, Johnson won a Senate seat. Many of his old opponents greeted him warmly when he arrived in Washington in March 1875. But Johnson's renewed career ended just after it began. In July, the ex-president traveled back to Tennessee for a visit with his daughter. On July 31, Johnson suffered a stroke and died at the age of sixty-six.

When Johnson returned to Washington in 1875 to serve in the Senate, he moved into a hotel. A friend observed that Johnson's new lodgings weren't as grand as the White House. "No," the former president replied, "but they are more comfortable." Less than six months later, Johnson was on his deathbed—a scene depicted in this lithograph. In his will, Johnson left this instruction for his burial: "Pillow my head with the Constitution of my country."

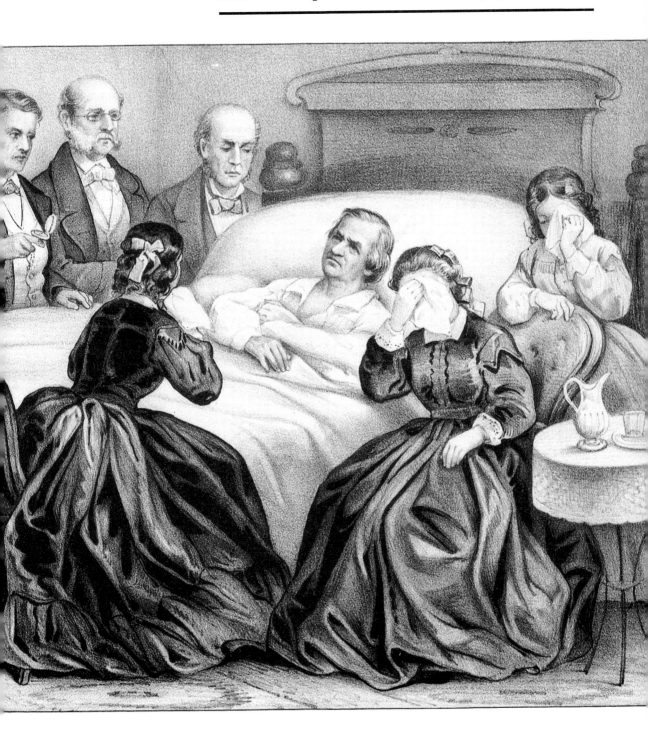

ULYSSES S. GRANT: EARLY YEARS

Ulysses S. Grant was born in Point Pleasant, Ohio, on April 27, 1822. His name at birth was Hiram Ulysses Grant. The change to Ulysses Simpson Grant was the result of a bookkeeping error at West Point, which the future president never bothered to correct.

Grant spent his boyhood in rural Ohio, working on his family's farm and helping out in the tannery, where his father made leather out of animal hides. He avoided the tannery when he could. Although Grant would later take part in some of the bloodiest battles in American history, he could never bear to see animals killed or hurt. A quiet, serious boy but not a particularly outstanding student, Grant was locally famous for his skill with horses.

In 1842, Grant's father, Jesse, won him an appointment to West Point. Grant had no desire for a military career, and at first he hated life at the academy. "If I could have escaped West Point without bringing myself into disgrace, I would have done so," Grant wrote in his memoirs. But he stayed on, graduating in 1843.

Grant's first post was at Jefferson Barracks in St. Louis, Missouri, where he served as infantry lieutenant. He began courting Julia Dent, the daughter of a local judge and the sister of Fred Dent, a West Point classmate.

Julia Dent is shown in this photograph (left) taken in her later years. She never looked directly at the camera when being photographed because she was embarrassed by her crossed eyes. This flaw didn't bother her devoted husband, who said her eyes were the same he "looked into when I first fell in love with you." As First Lady, Julia Grant was ahead of her time in many ways. She believed in women's suffrage—the movement to give women the vote—when it was still a radical idea. She was also personal friends with Susan B. Anthony, one of the pioneers of the women's rights movement.

This painting (below) shows the view of the Hudson River from the U.S. Military Academy at West Point, New York, in the nineteenth century. Grant's fellow West Point cadets included many of the men he would serve with in Mexico. Later, in the Civil War, Grant would fight against former classmates who threw in their lot with the Confederacy.

FROM THE
MEXICAN WAR
TO CIVILIAN LIFE

In 1846, Grant's regiment joined General Zachary Taylor's army in Texas. When tensions between the United States and Mexico turned into war, Grant first fought in northern Mexico. He then joined General Winfield Scott's army in its advance on Mexico City. Although his job as a quartermaster could have kept him out of combat, Grant fought in the front lines. His cool courage won him promotion to captain.

When the war ended, Grant returned to St. Louis and married Julia Dent. In 1852, two years after the birth of their first child, Grant was ordered to the West Coast. Bored and lonely without his family, the young officer turned to alcohol for comfort. In 1854, he had to resign his commission, at least in part because of his drinking. Historians still debate the extent of Grant's drinking problem, but charges of drunkenness (most of them unfounded) would follow him throughout his career.

Grant was soon reunited with his family, but the years ahead were a time of frustration and failure. Settling on a small piece of land in Missouri, he struggled to make a living by farming and selling wood. A string of business ventures all failed. By 1860, the Grants were living in Galena, Illinois, where Ulysses worked as a clerk in his family's leather shop.

Although Grant fought bravely in the Mexican War, he believed the conflict served only to win more land for slavery in the United States. In his memoirs, Grant called the war "one of the most unjust ever waged by a stronger against a weaker nation." This photograph (right) shows Lieutenant "Sam" Grant as he looked during the Mexican War. (The nickname was short for "Uncle Sam," itself a pun on his initials, "U. S.")

This Currier & Ives lithograph (below) depicts one of the key battles of the Mexican War: the American assault on Chapultepec Castle, a fortress blocking the way into Mexico City. Grant was brevetted (given a battlefield promotion) to captain for his role in the attack. James Longstreet, who fought alongside Grant in Mexico (and who later became one of the Confederacy's top generals), described Grant as "always cool, swift, and unhurried in battle . . . as unconcerned as if it were a hailstorm instead of a storm of bullets."

GRANT AND
THE CIVIL WAR

The Civil War rescued Grant from poverty and failure. Grant's friends persuaded the governor of Illinois to commission Grant a colonel and give him command of a regiment of the state's troops. Despite his short stature and plain manner, Grant proved an able leader. By 1862, Grant was a major general of volunteers. In February of that year, Grant became a national hero when he captured Fort Henry and Fort Donelson, two Confederate strongholds in Tennessee.

In April, however, Grant's forces nearly collapsed in a surprise Confederate attack near Shiloh Church at Pittsburg Landing, Tennessee. Grant rallied his troops and fought off the attack in a bloody two-day battle. After Shiloh, some Northern politicians accused Grant of drunkenness and incompetence and demanded that Lincoln fire him. The president refused, with the words "I cannot spare this man—he fights."

Grant now turned his attention to Vicksburg, the Confederacy's stronghold on the Mississippi River. After a long campaign ending in a six-week siege, the city's defenders surrendered on July 4, 1863. The president rewarded Grant with command of all Union troops between the Appalachian Mountains and the Mississippi. Later that fall a Confederate army was threatening to recapture Chattanooga, Tennessee, from Union forces. In November, Grant came to the area and drove out the Confederates.

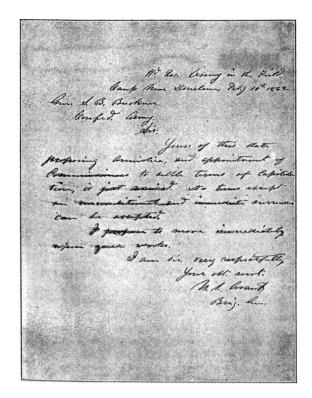

Grant sent this note (above) demanding "unconditional and immediate surrender" to General Simon Bolivar Buckner, commander of the Confederate forces holding Fort Donelson in Tennessee. Because "unconditional surrender" fit neatly with Grant's initials— "U. S."—the general gained a new nickname. The capture of Fort Donelson, with more than 12,000 prisoners, opened the way for the Union's capture of Nashville, and made Grant's reputation as a general.

Grant's newly won reputation was almost destroyed by the near-disaster at Shiloh two months later. At the end of the first day's fighting, the Union troops had been pushed back against the Tennessee River. During the battle, Grant personally rallied the soldiers, as shown in this print (right). As a cold rain drenched the battlefield, General William Tecumseh Sherman found Grant calmly standing under a tree. "Well, Grant, we've had the devil's own day, haven't we?" asked Sherman. With grim determination, Grant replied, "Yes, but we'll lick 'em tomorrow." True to his word, Grant forced the Confederates into retreat the following afternoon.

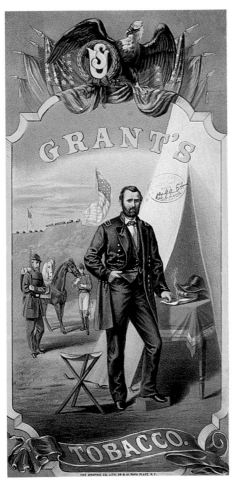

This poster, published during Grant's presidency, advertises "Grant's Tobacco." Grant was a smoker, but until the capture of Fort Donelson in 1862 he favored pipes. After a newspaper artist depicted Grant directing the battle with a cigar clenched between his teeth, admirers throughout the North sent the general cigars—as many as 10,000 boxes. Grant gave away some of the cigars, smoked the rest, and later wrote, "I have continued the habit ever since."

GENERAL IN CHIEF

After Grant's victories at Vicksburg and Chattanooga, Congress promoted him to lieutenant general—a rank last held by George Washington. In March 1864, Lincoln ordered Grant east to take command of the Union war effort. To the president's delight, the new commander outlined a bold plan to strike the Confederacy in as many places as possible.

In May, Grant led the Army of the Potomac into Virginia. Throughout the spring and summer, Grant's forces fought a series of bloody battles with Robert E. Lee's Army of Northern Virginia. Grant's forces suffered heavy casualties, and the general once again became a controversial figure. But Grant kept fighting.

Eventually, Grant's strategy paid off. After a long siege, the city of Petersburg fell on April 3, 1865. Richmond was captured a few days later. Grant pursued Lee's retreating army into Virginia, and on April 9, Lee surrendered at Appomattox Court House. As generous in victory as he was relentless in battle, Grant gave Lee liberal surrender terms and ordered his own men to share their rations with the starving Confederates.

A grateful nation heaped Grant with honors now that the war was over. Congress named him general of the armies; his hometown of Galena, Illinois, built a house for his family; and New York City gave him a cash gift of $105,000.

This lithograph (right) shows the scene in the parlor of Wilmer McLean's house in Appomattox, Virginia, when Grant and Robert E. Lee met to fix surrender terms on the afternoon of April 9, 1865. Lee arrived in his full-dress gray uniform, while Grant—always informal—showed up in a muddy private's uniform with general's stars pinned to the collar. When news of the surrender spread and Union troops began to cheer, Grant ordered them to stop, because, he said, "The rebels are our countrymen again."

Few people have gone from obscurity to worldwide fame in as short a time as Ulysses S. Grant. A few years before the Civil War, Grant and his family were living in this modest Missouri house (below), while Grant worked at odd jobs. By 1864, Grant was in command of the mightiest army in the world. Later that year, a movement to nominate Grant for the presidency began, but the general steadfastly refused to become a candidate. After the war, he said that the only political office he would consider would be the mayorship of Galena, Illinois. Then, said Grant, he could put in a sidewalk from his house to the train station.

GRANT TAKES OFFICE

After the war, Grant stayed on as general in chief of the U.S. Army. Although he wrote, "I certainly never had either ambition or taste for political life," the general soon found himself embroiled in the political battles of Reconstruction.

When President Andrew Johnson dismissed Secretary of War Edwin Stanton in 1867, he appointed Grant to take his place. Grant, however, served only briefly before turning the post back to Stanton. Grant's role in the controversy led the Republicans to see him as an ally. In May 1868 he won the party's nomination for the presidency, with Speaker of the House Schuyler Colfax as his running mate. Grant accepted the nomination with the words "Let us have peace," which became a memorable campaign slogan for the Republicans.

The Democrats chose Horatio Seymour, a former governor of New York, as their candidate. They raised the old question of Grant's drinking and attacked him for staying silent on many important issues. They also criticized the Republicans' Reconstruction policies, which they said would "Africanize" the South. For his part, Grant chose not to campaign, staying with his family in Galena while professional politicians drummed up votes.

Grant's personal popularity contributed to his victory in the election, as did the fact that many Democrats (including Seymour) had been only lukewarm supporters of the Union during the war.

Grant's Democratic opponent in 1868 was Horatio Seymour (1810–86; above), perhaps the most reluctant presidential candidate ever. The former New York governor did not want the job, but the party picked him anyway—he was the only candidate the different groups within the party could agree on. Republicans nicknamed him "the Great Decliner."

This lithograph (opposite, top) shows Grant and his family during the Civil War. On Grant's lap is Jesse Root Grant, born in 1858 and named for Grant's father. Seated behind the table are Ulysses Simpson Grant, Jr., born in 1852, and Frederick Dent Grant, born in 1850. Fred Grant, the general's eldest son, spent much of the Civil War alongside his father in the field. Next to Julia Grant is Nellie Wrenshall Grant, who was born in 1855.

"The Radical Party on a Heavy Grade" is the title of this cartoon (right), which shows Grant pulling a wagonload of the Republican Party's most radical members toward the White House. Although Grant didn't agree with many of the Radicals' policies, he became their ally during the crisis that led to Johnson's impeachment. Grant had at first accepted an appointment as secretary of war in the Johnson administration, but he soon resigned, allowing Edwin Stanton to return to the post.

GRANT AND RECONSTRUCTION

The most pressing problem facing the new president was Reconstruction. Unfortunately, Grant could not meet the challenge of easing the tensions between the South and the rest of the country while also protecting the newly won rights of the freed slaves.

In his inaugural address, Grant voiced his support for the Fifteenth Amendment, which guaranteed the vote to ex-slaves. The president also used federal troops to break up the Ku Klux Klan, a white supremacist group that terrorized Southern blacks. But by his second term, Grant seemed to lose interest in Reconstruction. When the governor of Louisiana reported that white mobs were attacking black voters, Grant telegraphed back that "the whole public [is] tired of these annual autumnal outbreaks of the South" and refused to send in troops.

Grant's style of leadership also came under attack. The president had always valued loyalty more than any other quality. For this reason, many of his cabinet and staff appointments went to old friends and military associates. Many of these men turned out to be incompetent or corrupt.

Despite these problems, Grant's popularity remained high in the election year of 1872. The Republicans nominated Grant for reelection, although a splinter group, the Liberal Republicans, supported Democratic challenger Horace Greeley, editor of the *New York Tribune*. Grant easily won a second term.

Grant's opponents tried to discredit his presidency by bringing up the old stories of his heavy drinking. This cartoon (above) from the election of 1868 shows Grant dancing a drunken jig in public. Grant was also accused of countless other sins, including "stupidity" and fathering illegitimate children. The Republicans weren't blameless, however. They portrayed Democratic candidate Horatio Seymour as a "traitor" for his sometimes lukewarm support of the Union during the Civil War.

One of the most important events of Grant's administration was the ratification of the Fifteenth Amendment on March 30, 1870. The amendment, adopted to protect the newly won political rights of the former slaves, states that "the right of citizens to vote . . . shall not be denied or abridged . . . on account of race, color, or previous condition of servitude"—meaning slavery. This print (right), showing the advances former slaves were making through education and skilled work, was published to commemorate the amendment's passage into law.

In 1870, a group of Republicans who favored milder Reconstruction policies toward the South formed the Liberal Republican Party. Two years later, the new party, along with the Democrats, nominated Horace Greeley, editor of the New York Tribune, for the presidency. Greeley was famous for his many eccentric ideas on a variety of subjects. Another newspaper editor described the election of 1872 as a choice between "a man of no ideas" (Grant) and "a man of too many" (Greeley). This poster shows Greeley and his running mate, Benjamin Gratz Brown.

CELEBRATION AT BALTIMORE ON MAY 19th 1870.

SCANDALS OF THE SECOND TERM

Many of the scandals that had simmered during Grant's first term boiled over in his second. Although no one questioned the president's personal honesty, his administration was filled with corruption.

The first major scandal to break was the Crédit Mobilier affair. Just before the election of 1872, newspaper reporters discovered that during the 1860s many congressmen had taken bribes of stock in the Crédit Mobilier of America, a false company set up by the Union Pacific Railroad. Among those who took bribes were Schuyler Colfax, Grant's first vice president, and Henry Wilson, his first running mate.

Next came the "Whiskey Ring" scandal. Grant's private secretary, Orville Babcock, was accused of helping whiskey distillers avoid paying taxes. Then Grant's secretary of war, William Belknap, was accused of selling licenses for trading on army posts and Indian reservations.

Grant wanted a third term, but the scandals, coupled with an economic depression starting in 1873, led the Republicans to pass him over in favor of Rutherford B. Hayes. In his last message to Congress, President Grant acknowledged his administration's shortcomings: "It was my fortune, or misfortune, to be called to the office of chief executive without any previous political training . . . Under such circumstances it is reasonable to suppose that errors of judgment must have occurred."

Schuyler Colfax (1823–85; above) was Grant's first vice president. In 1872, Colfax was among those caught in the Crédit Mobilier scandal. He was also found to have accepted a large bribe while Speaker of the House in the 1860s. In the election of 1872, the Republicans replaced Colfax with Massachusetts senator Henry Wilson. He died in 1875, leaving the nation without a vice president for the last year of Grant's presidency.

A cartoon (right) from the German-language edition of the humor magazine Puck shows Columbia—a symbol for the United States—as a "tattooed lady" covered in scandals. The corruption that plagued the Grant administration was only a large-scale version of the corruption in American politics and business in the late 1860s and 1870s.

Thomas Nast portrays President Grant falling into a barrel of scandals in this cartoon (right). Although Grant promised that corrupt officials would not go unpunished—"Let no guilty man escape," he once said— the president often defended friends convicted of wrongdoing.

Columbia : Wenn das Tätowiren in dieser Weise fortdauert, so muss ich trotz meiner guten Constitution zu Grunde gehen.

GRANT'S FINAL YEARS

Despite his troubled years in the White House, Grant was still a popular figure when he left office in March 1877. When the ex-president and his family set out on a two-year tour of the world, cheering crowds greeted them at every stop.

Back in the United States, however, Grant again experienced failure and frustration. After moving from Illinois to New York City, Grant invested his savings in Grant & Ward, an investment bank in which his son Frederick was a partner. The bank's director, Ferdinand Ward, swindled Grant out of his money, leaving the ex-president penniless.

Grant was now suffering from throat cancer, probably from decades of heavy cigar smoking. Knowing his death was imminent, Grant desperately wanted to provide financial security for his family. The famous writer Mark Twain generously offered Grant a contract for his memoirs. Fighting against time, the Grants moved to a cottage in Mount MacGregor, New York. There, Grant dictated for hours each day, finally writing in longhand after his voice failed.

Grant finished the book on July 19, 1885. Four days later, he died at the age of sixty-three. The general won his last battle: *The Personal Memoirs of U. S. Grant* earned $500,000 in royalties for Grant's family. Today, it is considered a classic of military history.

A photographer took this picture of Grant and his family as they prepared to tour a silver mine in Virginia City, Nevada, toward the end of their world tour in 1879. Grant's reputation was recovering by the end of the 1870s. There was even some talk in Republican circles that he would be a candidate for a third term in the election of 1880. Although Grant said he was "indifferent" to the idea of returning to the White House, he seemed to want the nomination. But the movement for a third term never got off the ground, and the Republican nomination went to James A. Garfield of Ohio.

This engraving (above) shows panicky investors on Wall Street after the failure of Grant & Ward in May 1884. The bank's collapse left Grant with about $200 to his name. "I have made it a rule of my life to trust a man long after other people gave him up," said Grant, "but I don't see how I can ever trust another human being again."

Desperate for money after the failure of Grant & Ward, the ex-president began writing articles on the Civil War for Century magazine. These articles led Mark Twain to persuade the Charles L. Webster publishing company to give Grant a contract for his memoirs. The book turned out to be a huge bestseller. A year after its publication, Grant's widow received this check (left) for $200,000.

By the summer of 1885, Grant was in constant pain from cancer. Unable to talk, he communicated by writing notes to his friends and family. One note, penned as death was near, said, "There never was one more willing to go than I am." This photograph (right) shows Grant wrapped in a blanket on the porch of his upstate New York cottage, working on his memoirs with the same determination and courage he displayed on the battlefields of two wars.

Grant lived in many places—Ohio, Missouri, Illinois, the White House—but his final resting place is in New York City, in this tomb (below) overlooking the Hudson River in Riverside Park. When Julia Grant died in 1902 at the age of seventy-seven, she was laid to rest at his side.

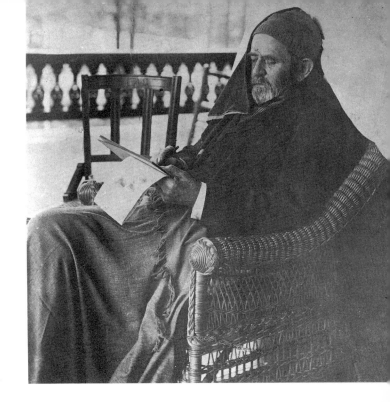

Resource Guide

Key to picture locations within the Library of Congress collections (and where available, photo negative numbers): P - Prints and Photographs Division; R - Rare Book Division; G - General Collections; MSS - Manuscript Division; G&M - Geography Division

PICTURES IN THIS VOLUME

2–3 army, P, USZ62-1731 4–5 music sheet, MSS 6–7 campaign poster, P 8–9 Map, G&M

Timeline: 10–11 Lincoln, P; riot, P, USZ62-28700 12–13 Richmond, P, B8171-3215; school,P, USZ62-8401 14–15 ticket, P; Ku Klux Klan, P, USZ62-31166; congressmen, P 16–17 cartoon, P, USZ62-29271; Yellowstone, P, USZ62-047670

Part I: 18–19 war scene, P 20–21 Lincoln, P, USZ62-23063; cabin, P, USZ62-10043 22–23 invitation, R 24–25 Mary Lincoln, P, USZ62-25789; family, P; house, P, USZ62-2071 26–27 poster, P, USZ62-11860; Frémont, P, USZ62-91388; young Lincoln, P, USZ62-12437 28–29 Douglas, P, USZ62-1754; debate, P, USZ62-29291 30–31 Lincoln, P; procession, P, USZ62-49814; cartoon, P 32–33 Hamlin, P; disguise, P, USZ62-8286; caricature, P, USZ62-13635; Capitol, P, USZ62-5062 34–35 conflict, P; Fort Sumter, P 36–37 cartoon, P; Davis, P 38–39 Bull Run, P; battle, P; army, P, USZ62-12453 40–41 Battle of New Orleans, P; Greeley, P, USZ62-1042; "Gunboat Candidate," P, USZ62-92038 42–43 R. Todd, P, USZ273-8244797; cabinet, P; Lincoln and son, P, USZ62-7990; Mary Lincoln, P, USZ62-13325 44–45 Emancipation Proclamation, P; Sojurner Truth, P, USZ62-16225 46–47 Lincoln, P, USZ62-4262; manuscript, P, USZ62-3118A; Round Top, P, USZC4-1004 48–49 Grant,

P "Soldier's Songs," USZ62-9637; Petersburg, P, B8171-931 50–51 poster, P; telegram, P, USZ62-7293; election of 1864, P 52–53 "Long Abraham," P, USZ62-8286; ball, P, USZ62-10246 54–55 Lincoln in Richmond, P, USZ62-2569; last portrait, P, USZ62-11896 56–57 wanted poster, P, USZ62-11193; assassination, P, USZ62-33804; escape, P, USZ62-14142 58–59 execution, P, LCB8171-7755; funeral, P; Higgins, P, USZ62-15047

Part II: 60–61 court house, P 62–63 Eliza Johnson, P, USZ62-25821; tailor shop, P, USZ62-31177 64–65 parade, P; portrait, P, USZ62-24824 66–67 dinner, P; death of Lincoln, P; oath, P, USZ62-10122 68–69 cartoon, P; House of Rep., P; Bureau, P, USZ62-18090 70–71 Stanton, P, USZ62-512; impeachment, P, USZ62-3433; Stevens, P, USZ62-22081 72–73 ticket, P, USZ62-9962; *Harper's*, P, USZ62-18089; Comm., P, USZ62-15341 74–75 death, P 76–77 J. Grant, P, USZ62-25799; West Point, P 78–79 Grant, P; battle scene, P 80–81 note, MSS; tobacco, P; Shiloh, P, USZ62-16852 82–83 mtg., P, USZ62-2480; home, P 84–85 Seymour, P; family, P; Radicals, P, USZ62-5992 86–87 cartoon, P; poster, P, USZ62-8035; 15th Am., P, USZ62-34936 88–89 Colfax, P, USZ62-34946; cartoon, P; Columbia, P, USZ62-34245; banquet, P 90–91 mine tour, P, USZ62-70526 92–93 market crash, P, USZ62-37326; check, P; old Grant, P, USZ62-7607; Grant's tomb, P

SUGGESTED READING

BLASSINGAME, WYATT. *The Look-It-Up Book of Presidents.* New York: Random House, 1984

DEGREGORIO, W. A. *The Complete Book of U.S. Presidents.* New York: Dembner Books, 1991.

SMITH, C. CARTER, ed. *One Nation Again.* Brookfield, CT: The Millbrook Press, 1993.

SMITH, C. CARTER, ed. *1863: The Crucial Year.* Brookfield, CT: The Millbrook Press, 1993.

WHITNEY, D. C. *The American Presidents,* 6th ed. New York: Doubleday, 1986.

WILLS, GARRY. *Lincoln at Gettysburg.* New York: Simon & Schuster, 1992.

Index

Page numbers in *italics* indicate illustrations